Arthur Rio

A Portrait of t
as a Young Man

Based on the book by
James Joyce

methuen | drama
LONDON • NEW YORK • OXFORD • NEW DELHI • SYDNEY

METHUEN DRAMA

Bloomsbury Publishing Plc

50 Bedford Square. London WC1B 3DP. UK

1385 Broadway, New York, NY 10018, USA

BLOOMSBURY, METHUEN DRAMA and the Methuen Drama logo
are trade marks of Bloomsbury Publishing Plc

First published in Great Britain 2018

Cover design: Toby Way

Cover image © Ste Murray

A catalogue record for this book is available from the British Library.

A catalog record for this book is available from the Library of Congress.

ISBN: PB: 978-1-350-09682-0
ePDF: 978-1-350-09684-4
eBook: 978-1-350-09683-7

Series: Modern Plays

Typeset by Country Setting, Kingdown, Kent CT14 8ES
Printed and bound in Great Britain

ROUGH

MAGIC

A Portrait of the Artist as a Young Man

written by James Joyce
adapted for the stage by Arthur Riordan
directed by Ronan Phelan

This adaptation of *A Portrait of the Artist as a Young Man*
was originally commissioned by Abbey Theatre
Amharclann na Mainistreach. It was produced
by Rough Magic Theatre Company and premiered at
Pavilion Theatre, Dún Laoghaire on 28 September 2018
as part of Dublin Theatre Festival.

A Portrait of the Artist as a Young Man
by James Joyce
adapted for the stage by Arthur Riordan

All the roles were played by members of the ensemble.
They were, in alphabetical order:

Martha Breen
Amy Conroy
Peter Corboy
Aoibhéann McCann
Karen McCartney
Paul Mescal
Conor O'Riordan
Kieran Roche

Director	Ronan Phelan
Set and Costume Design	Katie Davenport
Lighting Design	Sarah Jane Shiels
Sound Design	
and Composition	Denis Clohessy
Movement Director	Emma O'Kane
Design Assistant	Florentina Burcea
Assistant Director	Ciara Elizabeth Smyth
Production Manager	Rob Furey
Stage Managers	Anne Layde
	Cian Mulhall
Chief LX	Tomek Rola
Producers	Selina O'Reilly
	Gemma Reeves
PR Consultant	Conleth Teevan
Graphic Design	Stu Bradfield
Production Photography	Ste Murray

Ronan Phelan   *Director*

For Rough Magic: *Assassins* (Rough Magic SEEDS); *The Effect* and *Mr Burns* (Rough Magic SEEDS).

Ronan is a freelance theatre director based in Dublin. He was recently appointed Associate Director at Rough Magic Theatre Company and has completed a year as Resident Assistant Director at the Abbey Theatre, Dublin.

Previous directing credits include: *Annie* (Cork Opera House); *Much Ado About Nothing* (Lir Academy); *Before Monsters Were Made* (national tour); *Inhabitance* (Glassdoll Productions); *To Space* (Niamh Shaw); *Lambo* and *Clear_the_Air* (Underscore_ Productions); *Broadening* (Glassdoll Productions); *Pocket Music* (Dublin Fringe 2011, winner Little Gem Award) and *Durang Durang* (Brazen Tales Theatre Company).

Radio productions include: *Lambo* (RTÉ Drama on One, winner PPI Radio Awards Best Drama 2014).

Ronan is a former participant of the Rough Magic SEEDS programme and is a graduate of the DIT Conservatory of Music and Drama.

Arthur Riordan   *Writer*

Arthur Riordan is a playwright and actor, and a founder member of Rough Magic.

Arthur's writing includes the libretto for Andrew Synnott's *Dubliners* opera (for Opera Theatre Company and Wexford Festival Opera), the book and lyrics for the musical *The Train* (for Rough Magic, music by Bill Whelan), an adaptation of Ibsen's *Peer Gynt* (for Rough Magic, music by Tarab), a stage adaptation of Flann O'Brien's *Slattery's Sago Saga* (for The Performance Corporation), the multi-award-winning musical *Improbable Frequency* (for Rough Magic, music by Conor Kelly and Sam Park), *Hidden Charges*, and a one-man show, *The Emergency Session* (also for Rough Magic); as well as *Love Me?!* (for The Corn Exchange), and two collaborations with Des Bishop – *Rap Éire* (for Bickerstaffe), and *Shooting Gallery* (for Bedrock Productions).

Katie Davenport *Set and Costume Design*

For Rough Magic: *A Midsummer Night's Dream* directed by Lynne Parker for the 2018 Kilkenny Arts Festival.

Katie is a Set and Costume Designer who trained in Production Design for Stage and Screen at IADT. After graduating in 2014, she worked as an associate designer at the Lyric, the Abbey, Galway Arts Festival and the Gaiety Theatre. In 2017, she was Designer-in-Residence at the Gate Theatre. Katie has designed for directors Selina Cartmell, Graham McLaren, Oonagh Murphy, Ronan Phelan, Lynne Parker, Tom Creed, Ben Barnes and Dan Colley. Recent artistic achievements include representing Ireland at Evolving Design for Performance, an exhibition of European Theatre Design (Beijing NCPA, 2016) and receiving a prestigious ICAD award for art direction for iD Mobile's TV ads (2016). She has also worked as assistant designer in film and TV for Ardmore Studios, RTE, PBS and Sky Arts and is a committee member of ISSSD (Irish Society of Stage and Screen Designers). She is currently designing *Tales of Hoffmann* for Irish National Opera.

Sarah Jane Shiels *Lighting Design*

For Rough Magic: *A Midsummer Night's Dream*, *The Effect*, *How to Keep an Alien* (Sonya Kelly/Rough Magic); *Everything Between Us*, *The Critic*, *The House Keeper* and *Plaza Suite*.

Sarah Jane is a freelance theatre designer. She began lighting at Dublin Youth Theatre, completing a BA in Drama and Theatre Studies 2006 at Trinity College Dublin and Rough Magic SEEDS 2006–2008. Since 2010 she has been co-artistic director of WillFredd Theatre.

Recent designs include: *Frnknstn* (Theatre Lovett); *Dolores*, *Soldier Still*, *Dusk Ahead* (Junk Ensemble); *Nora* (Corn Exchange); *Radio Rosario* (Little John Nee); *Jimmy's Hall* (Abbey Theatre); *Educating Rita* (Lyric Theatre); *Dublin Oldschool* (Project Arts Centre); *The Remains of Maisie Duggan* (Abbey Theatre); *Town is Dead* (Abbey Theatre); *Lessness* (TheEmergencyRoom); BEES!, *Jockey*, CARE, *Farm*, *Follow* (WillFredd Theatre); PALS (winner Irish Times Theatre Award Best Lighting, 2015); *The Boys of Foley*

Street, Laundry, World's End Lane, Basin (ANU Productions); *It Folds* (Junk Ensemble/Brokentalkers, winner IrishTimes Theatre Award Best Lighting, 2015); *This Beach, Have I No Mouth, The Blue Boy* and *Silver Stars* (Brokentalkers).

Denis Clohessy   *Sound Design and Composition*

For Rough Magic: *A Midsummer Night's Dream, Famished Castle, Assassins, Attempts on Her Life, The Importance of Being Earnest, Don Carlos* and *Sodome My Love,* for which he won an Irish Times Theatre Award.

Other Irish dance and theatre companies he has worked with include the Abbey Theatre, the Gate Theatre, Fishamble, Junk Ensemble, Fabulous Beast and Corn Exchange. He was nominated for an Irish Times Theatre Award in 2015 (for Junk Ensemble and Brokentalker's *It Folds*), and was an associate artist with the Abbey in 2008. Denis was a participant on Rough Magic's ADVANCE programme in 2012. Last year Pat Kinevane's play *Silent* (Fishamble) for which Denis composed the music won an Olivier award

His work in film and television includes: music for the feature films *Older than Ireland* (Snack Box Films); *The Irish Pub* (Atom Films); *His and Hers* (Venom Film); *The Land of the Enlightened* (Savage Film); *In View* (Underground Cinema); *The Reluctant Revolutionary* (Underground Films); and the television series *Limits of Liberty* (South Wind Blows) performed by the RTÉ Concert Orchestra.

Martha Breen

For Rough Magic: *A Midsummer Night's Dream* directed by Lynne Parker for the 2018 Kilkenny Arts Festival.

Martha is a recent graduate of the Lir Academy (2018). During her time there she appeared in *The Caucasian Chalk Circle* directed by Tom Creed, *The Winter's Tale* directed by Nona Shepphard, *La Ronde* directed by Lynne Parker, *Merrily We Roll Along* directed by Ronan Phelan and *Incognito* directed by Ronan Leahy. She was also directed in her Lir Academy showcase by Annabelle Comyn, and in their short film series by Conor McMahon. Martha was a member of Dublin Youth Theatre and performed with them in the Dublin Theatre Festival in *Spring Awakening* directed by Gyuri Vidovsky and *I've to Mind Her* by Shaun Dunne, directed by Gary Keegan.

Amy Conroy

For Rough Magic: *A Midsummer Night's Dream* directed by Lynne Parker for the 2018 Kilkenny Arts Festival.

Amy Conroy is an actor, playwright and Artistic Director of HotForTheatre. Her first radio play, *Hold This*, was recorded and broadcast on RTÉ Radio One in September 2010. Her first stage play, *I ♥ Alice ♥ I*, won the Fishamble Award for New Writing in the 2010 Dublin Fringe Festival and has played at the Ulster Bank Dublin Theatre Festival; the Peacock stage of the Abbey Theatre; the Irish Arts Centre in New York; Lókal Festival, Iceland; Glasgay Festival in Glasgow; Brisbane, Auckland Arts Festival; Ten Days on the Island Festival, Tasmania; Queer Theatre Festival Croatia; Centre Culturel Irlandai, Paris; and The Lyric Theatre Belfast. It was broadcast on RTÉ Radio One, has been translated and performed in Poland, Italy and Iceland and is published by Oberon.

Her second show, *Eternal Rising of the Sun*, won the Best Female Performer Award at Dublin Fringe Festival and a nomination for Best Actress in the *Irish Times* Theatre Awards 2011. *Eternal Rising of the Sun* has played at the Dublin Theatre Festival 2012 and Fringe World in Perth, Australia.

In September 2013 HotForTheatre presented *Break* in Project Arts Centre. *Luck Just Kissed You Hello* premiered at the Galway International Arts Festival in 2015, and played at the Dublin Theatre Festival later that year. It was nominated for Best New Play in the *Irish Times* Theatre Awards 2016.

Amy has performed most recently in a critically acclaimed production of *The Taming of the Shrew* at Shakespeare's Globe, London, directed by Caroline Byrne; *Futureproof*, directed by Tom Creed; Martin Sharry's *Playboyz* in the Dublin Theatre Festival 2017; *My Son My Son*, directed by Veronica Dyas; and *A Day In May*, directed by Gerry Stembridge. She directed *Me Sara* (*Priming the Canon*) for the Abbey Theatre; *Looking Deadly* (Dublin Fringe –

national tour); and *Here and Now* by Veronica Dyas, performed as part of Thisispopbaby's *Where We Live* Festival.

Peter Corboy

For Rough Magic: *The Critic, Assassins* and *Mr Burns* (*Rough Magic SEEDS*) and most recently *A Midsummer Night's Dream* directed by Lynne Parker for the 2018 Kilkenny Arts Festival.

Peter is a graduate of Trinity College Dublin's BA in Drama and Theatre Studies. Previous credits include *Everything Not Saved* (MALAPROP); *The Water Orchard* (Collapsing Horse); *Outlying Islands* (Sugarglass Theatre and Columbia University, New York); *Our Island* (Mirari Productions); *Far Away from Me* (The Ark) and *Ethica* (Sugarglass Theatre, Trinity College Dublin and NATFIZ Sofia). He has performed as part of the Dublin Fringe (*At Sea, The Last Post, Anna in Between*); Galway Fringe (*This is the Day*); Irish Student Drama Awards (*Life in Our Blood*); the Enniskillen Beckett Festival and Dublin Theatre Festival.

Aoibhéann McCann

For Rough Magic: *A Midsummer Night's Dream* directed by Lynne Parker for the 2018 Kilkenny Arts Festival.

Other theatre credits include: *The Great Gatsby, Assassins* (Gate Theatre); *Coast, Harder Faster More, Wrapped* (Red Bear Productions); *Stars in the Morning Sky* (Belgrade Theatre, Coventry); *Ourselves Alone* (Just Theatre, Camden); *Much Ado About Nothing, The Taming of the Shrew* (Fortune's Fool/Iveagh Gardens); *Holes* (Company of Angels); *The Folk Contraption* (Vault Festival, Old Vic); *Suddenly Last Summer* (Hampstead Theatre/Drama).

Film/television includes: *Vikings: Season 6* (MGM, History); *Can't Cope Won't Cope 2, A Terrible Beauty* (RTE); *The Midnight Court, Cumann na mBan 100* (TG4); *Soulsmith* (Whim Productions); *The Break, Gustav* (Stanley's Deathpark Productions); *Street Spirit* (Bailey Films).

Radio includes: *Wrapped, Harder Faster More* (RTÉ); *William Melville, Matches, Yummy Mummy* (Henchman Productions/Newstalk).

Aoibhéann trained at the Oxford School of Drama.

Karen McCartney

For Rough Magic: *The Train*, *Mr Burns* (*Rough Magic SEEDS*) and most recently *A Midsummer Night's Dream* directed by Lynne Parker for the 2018 Kilkenny Arts Festival.

Karen was part of the first group to graduate from the BA in Acting course at the Lir Academy in 2014. Since then, she has gone on to work at Druid Theatre Company on DruidShakespeare and *Big Maggie*, at the Gate Theatre on *The Heiress* and *Jacques Brel is Alive and Well and Living in Paris*. She was also part of the cast of *Hostel 16* for the Dublin Fringe Festival and *Signatories* at the Olympia Theatre. She played Serena, a mermaid, in *Futureproof* as part of Cork Midsummer Festival.

Paul Mescal

For Rough Magic: *A Midsummer Night's Dream* directed by Lynne Parker for the 2018 Kilkenny Arts Festival.

Paul is a graduate of the Lir Academy. His theatre credits include: *The Great Gatsby* and *The Red Shoes* (Gate Theatre); *The Plough and the Stars* (Lyric Hammersmith/Abbey Theatre); *Asking for It* (Landmark/Everyman/Abbey Theatre). He has also appeared in the short film *Happyish*, directed by Juanita Wilson.

Conor O'Riordan

For Rough Magic: *Mr Burns* (Rough Magic SEEDS) and *A Midsummer Night's Dream* directed by Lynne Parker for the 2018 Kilkenny Arts Festival.

Conor is a recent graduate of the Lir Academy. His theatre credits include: Umbrella Theatre Project's *Glowworm*, directed by Davey Kelleher.

Kieran Roche

For Rough Magic: *Way to Heaven* (Rough Magic SEEDS) and *A Midsummer Night's Dream* directed by Lynne Parker for the 2018 Kilkenny Arts Festival.

Kieran is a graduate of the Gaiety School of Acting two-year full-time programme. His work includes: *The Birthday Man* with the Gonzo Theatre Company, *Tactics* with Sickle Moon Theatre Company and *Walkinstown* with Monkey Backstage Theatre Company.

Kieran is also a member of the sketch comedy group Rocket Octopus, who premiered their first show *Things We Talk About When We Talk About Things* in May 2018.

About Rough Magic

Since its foundation in 1984, Rough Magic has become a company of continual regeneration, evolving around the principle that it is part of a world culture that celebrates Irish identity diverse in nature and outward-looking in its vision. It has delivered over fifty Irish premieres, the debuts of many theatre-makers, and the pioneering SEEDS programme.

The company policy has three strands: commissioning new Irish work, innovative productions from the classical repertoire and contemporary international writing. Based in Dublin, Rough Magic regularly performs at Project Arts Centre and other major venues, touring Ireland, the UK and beyond, garnering many awards at home and abroad.

This year we bring Joyce, the great modernist architect of language, on a national odyssey. *A Portrait of the Artist as a Young Man*, presented first for the Dublin Theatre Festival and then on tour around Ireland; in an adaptation by founder member Arthur Riordan, directed by Associate Director and SEEDS graduate Ronan Phelan, with a creative ensemble comprising dynamic emerging talent with award-winning, established artists.

Rough Magic is connected across the full spectrum of theatre activity and creative practice. Our aim is firstly to make great theatre, but also to advance and contribute to the cultural life of Ireland. The company will continue to put the artist at the centre of our production and development strategies; to strengthen our position as a national company that responds to all parts of the island; and to form supportive partnerships with organisations and individuals who share our sense of the value of art in general, and theatre in particular, in offering a new vision for the nation.

Artistic Director	Lynne Parker
General Manager	Gemma Reeves
Producer	Selina O'Reilly
Associate Director/SEEDS Curator	Ronan Phelan
Finance Officer	Daniel O'Brien
Marketing and Communications	Aileen Power

A Portrait of the Artist as a Young Man

To my late father
Niall O'Riordan

Characters

Stephen 1

Narrator 1

Simon Dedalus, *Stephen's father*

May Dedalus, *Stephen's mother*

Eileen, *a young girl; a neighbour and friend of Stephen's*

Wells, Roche, Fleming, Athy, *students at Clongowes*

Fr Arnall, Fr Doran, The Rector, *teachers and staff at Clongowes*

Mr Casey, *a friend of Simon's*

Emma, *a family friend, and for several years Stephen's muse*

Stephen 2

Narrator 2

Note: here, and as a general rule, the new Stephen is the former Narrator, thus Narrator 1 becomes Stephen 2. Other characters will also occasionally narrate.

Mr Tate, *a priest: teacher at Belvedere College*

Heron, Boland, Ennis, Boy, *students at Belvedere*

Stephen 3

Narrator 3

A Porter, *at Queen's University Cork*

Auctioneer

Barman

Maurice, *Stephen's younger brother.*

Four Girls *in the brothel district*

Stephen 4

Narrator 4

Old Woman

Priest *at confession*

Director of Studies, *a priest at Belvedere College*

Three Bathers *at Dollymount*

'Bird Girl' *at Dollymount*

Stephen 5

Narrator 5

Stephen's Sister

Davin, Cranly, McCann, Temple, Lynch, *colleagues of Stephen's at University*

Flower Girl *on Grafton Street*

Dean of Studies *at Queen's College Dublin*

Father Moran, *an Irish-language enthusiast*

Two Students *passing by*

Plus other nameless
Schoolboys, Students, Passers-by *and disembodied* **Voices**

For most of the play there is a Narrator onstage, watching Stephen, commenting, and often speaking Stephen's thoughts. At intervals, as Stephen grows older, the actor playing Stephen is replaced as Stephen by the actor playing the Narrator, and a new Narrator appears, who will eventually replace the current Stephen, etc., thus a sort of relay of Stephens/Narrators is created.

Act One

Prologue

Simon *and* **Stephen 1** *appear.*

Simon   Once upon a time and a very good time it was there was a moocow coming down along the road and this moocow that was coming down along the road met a nicens little boy named baby Tuckoo . . .

Narrator 1   His father told him that story.

Stephen 1   His father looked at him through a glass: he had a hairy face. He was baby Tuckoo. The moocow came down the road where Betty Byrne lived: she sold lemon platt. When you wet the bed first it is warm then it gets cold.

May *appears.*

Stephen 1   His mother put on the oilsheet. That had the queer smell. His mother had a nicer smell than his father. Dante had two brushes in her press.

Dante *appears. She holds up two brushes.*

Dante   The brush with the maroon velvet back is for Michael Davitt and the brush with the green velvet back is for Parnell.

Stephen 1 (*sings*)   O the green wose botheth, the green wose botheth – the Vances lived in number seven. They had a different father and mother. They were Eileen's father and mother.

Narrator 1   When they were grown up he was going to marry Eileen.

Eileen *appears. She and* **Stephen** *dance and run around.* **Stephen** *bumps into* **Dante**.

May   Stephen! O, Stephen will apologise.

Dante   O, if not, the eagles will come and pull out his eyes.

Stephen 1 and **Eileen** (*sing*)
Pull out his eyes
Apologise,
Apologise,
Pull out his eyes.
Apologise,
Pull out his eyes.

May   Now, you won't speak to the rough boys, will you
Stephen?

Stephen 1   No.

Narrator 1   He pretended not to see that she was going
to cry. She was a nice mother but she was not so nice when
she cried.

Simon   Here, Stephen. Ten shillings. And if there's
anything you want, write to me.

Stephen 1   I will.

Simon   Goodbye. And Stephen . . . whatever you do, never
peach on a fellow.

Stephen 1   No.

Simon/May   Goodbye, Stephen, goodbye! Goodbye,
Stephen, goodbye!

Scene One

Clonglowes. Nasty **Roche** *appears.*

Roche   What is your name?

Stephen 1   Stephen Dedalus.

Roche   What kind of a name is that? What is your father?

Now **Wells** *and* **Fleming** *appear too.*

Stephen 1 A gentleman.

Roche Is he a magistrate?

Wells Tell us, Dedalus, do you kiss your mother before you go to bed?

Stephen 1 I do.

Wells O, I say, here's a fellow says he kisses his mother every night before he goes to bed.

Stephen 1 I do not.

Wells O, I say, here's a fellow says he doesn't kiss his mother before he goes to bed.

Narrator 1 Wells shouldered him into the square ditch because Stephen wouldn't swop his little snuff box for Wells's seasoned hacking chestnut, the conqueror of forty.

Fleming That was a mean thing to do, Wells.

Roche I saw a big rat jump plop into the scum in that ditch.

Narrator 1 The cold slime of the ditch covered his whole body.

Fleming What's up? Have you a pain or what's up with you?

Stephen 1 I don't know.

Fleming Sick in your breadbasket, because your face looks white. It will go away.

Narrator 1 But he was not sick there. He thought he was sick in his heart if you could be sick in that place. Christmas vacation was very far away: but one time it would come because the earth moved round always, a big ball in the middle of clouds.

Stephen *writes in his geography book.*

Stephen 1   Stephen Dedalus. Class of Elements. Clongowes Wood College. Sallins. County Kildare. Ireland. Europe. The World. The Universe.

Narrator 1   What was after the universe? It was very big to think about everything and everywhere. Only God could do that. It pained him that he did not know where the universe ended. His bed was very hot and his face and body were very hot.

Lights up. It's morning.

Fleming   He's sick.

Roche   Who is?

Fleming   I'll tell McGlade you're not well.

Wells   Get Simon Moonan to go – he's McGlade's suck.

Narrator 1   Suck was a queer word. Once he washed his hands in the lavatory of the Wicklow Hotel and his father pulled the stopper up by the chain after and the dirty water went down through the hole in the basin. It had made a sound like that: suck. To remember the white look of the lavatory made him feel cold and then hot.

Wells   Dedalus, don't spy on us, sure you won't? I didn't mean to. Sure you won't?

Stephen 1   I won't.

Wells   I didn't mean to, honour bright. It was only for cod. I'm sorry.

Narrator 1   His father had told him, whatever he did –

Stephen 1   – never to peach on a fellow.

Fleming   He's sick, he's not foxing.

Father Arnall *appears, gives* **Stephen** *a cup.*

Father Arnall   We must pack off to the infirmary because we have the collywobbles!

Narrator 1   Father Arnall was very decent to say that. That was all to make him laugh. But he could not laugh because his cheeks and lips were all shivery.

Father Arnall   Drink this up, it's beef tea,

Narrator 1   That was the infirmary. He *was* sick then.

Athy   Hello! It's young Dedalus! What's up?

Father Arnall   The sky is up. You'll get your walking papers in the morning when the doctor comes.

Athy   Will I? I'm not well yet.

Father Arnall   You'll get your walking papers. I tell you.

He exits.

Narrator 1   Had they written home to tell his mother and father? Or he would write a letter for the priest to bring.

Stephen 1   Dear Mother,

I am sick. I want to go home. Please come and take me home. I am in the infirmary.

Your fond son, Stephen.

Narrator 1   There was cold sunlight outside the window. You could die just the same on a sunny day.

Stephen 1   He might die before his mother came.

Narrator 1   All the fellows would be at the mass, dressed in black, all with sad faces.

Wells   Wells too would be there but no fellow would look at him.

Fleming   And Wells would be sorry then for what he had done.

Narrator 1   And the bell would toll slowly.

A Voice
    Ding dong, the castle bell
    Farewell my mother.

> Bury me in the old churchyard
> Beside my eldest brother.
> My coffin shall be black
> Six angels at my back
> Two to sing and two to pray
> And two to carry me away.

Narrator 1   He wanted to cry quietly but not for himself: for the words, so beautiful and sad, like music.

Athy   You have a queer name, Dedalus, and I have a queer name too, Athy. My name is the name of a town. Your name is like Latin. Are you good at riddles?

Stephen 1   Not very good.

Athy   Why is the county of Kildare like the leg of a fellow's breeches?

Stephen 1   I give it up.

Athy   Because there is a thigh in it. Do you see the joke? Athy is the town in the county Kildare and a thigh is the other thigh.

Stephen 1   Oh, I see.

Athy   That's an old riddle. You know, you can ask that riddle another way.

Stephen 1   Can you?

Athy   The same riddle. Do you know the other way to ask it?

Stephen 1   No.

Athy   Can you not think of the other way? There is another way but I won't tell you what it is.

He ostentatiously opens a newspaper.

Now it is all about politics in the papers. Do your people talk about that too?

Stephen 1   Yes. My father is on one side. Dante is on the other. She says Parnell is a bad man. My mother is on no side.

Athy   It says here that Parnell is dead.

Wells   The fire rose and fell on the wall. It was like waves.

Simon, **Dante** *and others appear.*

Narrator 1   He saw the sea of waves, long dark waves rising and falling, rising and falling.

Narrator *repeats 'rising and falling' under the next three lines.*

Simon   Dark under the moonless night.

Rising and falling.

Dante   A tiny light twinkled at the pierhead where the ship was entering –

Rising and falling.

Simon   A voice of sorrow came over the waters.

Rising and falling.

We hear voices, mingled with **Stephen**'*s feverish breathing.*

Father Arnall   He is dead.

Simon   He is dead.

Rising and falling.

Father Arnall   We saw him lying upon the catafalque.

Athy   A wail of sorrow went up from the people.

Simon   A multitude of people gathered by the water's edge to see the ship that was entering their harbour.

Narrator 1   Parnell!

Dante   Parnell!

Simon   He is dead!

Dante   He is dead!

All   He is dead!

Scene Two

Narrator 1   A great fire, banked high and red, flamed in the grate and under the ivy-twined branches of the chandelier the Christmas table was spread.

Stephen *is sitting at a table set for Christmas dinner, with* **Simon, May, Mr Casey,** *and* **Dante.**

Simon   Yes. Well now, that's all right. O, we had a good walk, hadn't we, John? Yes . . . I wonder if there's any likelihood of dinner this evening . . . What are you laughing at, you little puppy you? Yes . . . We got a good breath of ozone round the Head today. Ay, bedad. You didn't stir out at all, Mrs Riordan?

Dante   No.

Simon   A thimbleful, John, just to whet your appetite.

May   Sit over.

Simon   Now, Mrs Riordan, sit over. John, sit you down, my hearty. Now, Stephen.

Stephen 1   Bless us, O Lord, and these Thy gifts which of Thy bounty we are about to receive through Christ our Lord. Amen.

Simon   Amen.

Narrator 1   Clongowes was far away: the warm heavy smell of turkey and ham and celery rose from the plates and dishes and the great fire was banked high and red in the grate and the green ivy and red holly made you feel so happy.

May   Simon, you haven't given Mrs Riordan any sauce.

Simon   Haven't I? Mrs Riordan, pity the poor blind.

Dante   No, thanks.

Simon   How are you off, John?

Mr Casey   I'm all right. Go on yourself.

Simon   May? Here, Stephen, here's something to make your hair curl.

Narrator 1   It was his first Christmas dinner with the adults. His little brothers and sisters were waiting in the nursery, as he had often waited, till the pudding came.

Simon   That was a good answer our friend made to the canon. What?

Mr Casey   I didn't think he had that much in him.

Simon   'I'll pay your dues, Father, when you cease turning the house of God into a polling booth!'

Dante   A nice answer for any man calling himself a Catholic to give to his priest.

Mr Casey   We go to the house of God in all humility to pray to our Maker and not to hear election addresses.

Dante   A priest would not be a priest if he did not tell his flock what is right and what is wrong.

May   For pity sake and for pity sake, let us have no political discussion on this day of all days in the year.

Simon   Yes, yes. Now then, who's for more turkey?

Dante   Nice language for any Catholic to use!

May   Mrs Riordan, I appeal to you to let the matter drop now.

Dante   And am I to sit here and listen to the pastors of my church being flouted?

Simon   Nobody is saying a word against them, so long as they don't meddle in politics.

Mr Casey   Let them leave politics alone, or the people may leave their church alone.

Dante   You hear?

May   Mr Casey! Simon! Let it end now.

Simon   What? Were we to desert him at the bidding of the English people?

Dante   He was no longer worthy to lead. He was a public sinner.

Mr Casey   We are all sinners and black sinners.

Dante   Woe be to the man by whom scandal cometh! It would be better for him that a millstone were tied around his neck and that he were cast into the depths of the sea rather than that he should scandalise one of these, my least little ones. That is the language of the Holy Ghost.

Simon   And very bad language if you ask me.

May (*indicates* **Stephen**)   Simon!

Simon   Yes, yes. I meant about the . . . I was thinking about the bad language of the railway porter. Here, Stephen, show me your plate, old chap. Eat away now. Here . . . There's a tasty bit here we call the pope's nose. If any lady or gentleman . . . Well, you can't say but you were asked. Well now, the day kept up fine after all. There were plenty of strangers down too . . . I think there were more strangers down than last Christmas . . . Well, my Christmas dinner has been spoiled anyhow.

Dante   There could be neither luck nor grace, in a house where there is no respect for the pastors of the Church. O, he'll remember all this when he grows up – the language he heard against God and religion and priests in his own home.

Mr Casey   Let him remember, too, the language with which the priests and the priests' pawns broke Parnell's heart and hounded him into his grave. Let him remember that too when he grows up.

Simon   Sons of bitches! When he was down they turned on him to betray him and rend him like rats in a sewer. Low-lived dogs!

Dante   They behaved rightly. They obeyed their bishops and their priests.

May   Well, it is perfectly dreadful to say that not even for one day in the year can we be free from these dreadful disputes!

Dante   I will not say nothing. I will defend my Church and my religion when it is insulted and spit on by renegade Catholics.

Mr Casey   Tell me, did I tell you that story about a very famous spit?

Simon   You did not, John.

Mr Casey   Why then, it is a most instructive story. It happened not long ago in the County Wicklow where we are now. And I may tell you, ma'am, that I, if you mean me, am no renegade Catholic. I am a Catholic as my father was and his father before him and his father before him again, when we gave up our lives rather than sell our faith.

Dante   The more shame to you now, to speak as you do.

Simon (*sings*)
     O, come all you Roman Catholics
     That never went to Mass.

Narrator 1   Why was Mr Casey against the priests? Dante must be right then.

Stephen 1   But he had heard his father say that she was a spoiled nun.

Narrator 1   Perhaps that made her severe against Parnell.

Stephen 1   Dante did not like him to play with Eileen because Eileen was a Protestant.

Simon   Let us have the story, John. It will help us to digest.

Mr Casey   The story is very short and sweet. It was one day down in Arklow, a cold bitter day, not long before the chief died. May God have mercy on him!

Simon   Before he was killed, you mean.

Mr Casey   We were down there at a meeting and after the meeting was over we had to make our way to the railway station through the crowd. Such booing and baaing, man, you never heard. They called us all the names in the world. Well, there was one old lady, and a drunken old harridan she was surely, that paid all her attention to me. She kept dancing along beside me in the mud bawling and screaming into my face: 'Priest hunter! Kitty O'Shea!'

Simon   And what did you do, John?

Mr Casey   I let her bawl away. It was a cold day and to keep up my heart I had (saving your presence, ma'am) a quid of Tullamore in my mouth and sure I couldn't say a word in any case because my mouth was full of tobacco juice.

Simon   Well, John?

Mr Casey   Well. I let her bawl away, to her heart's content, Kitty O'Shea and the rest of it, till at last she called that lady a name that I won't sully this Christmas board nor your ears, ma'am, nor my own lips by repeating.

Simon   And what did you do, John?

Mr Casey   Do! She stuck her ugly old face up at me when she said it and I had my mouth full of tobacco juice. I bent down to her and phth! says I to her like that, right into her eye. 'O Jesus Mary and Joseph!' says she. 'I'm blinded! I'm blinded and drownded!' (*Coughing and laughter.*) 'I'm blinded entirely!'

Dante   Very nice! Ha! Very nice!

Simon   Ah, John. It is true for them. We are an unfortunate priest-ridden race and always were and always will be till the end of the chapter. A priest-ridden godforsaken race!

Dante   They are the apple of God's eye. Touch them not, says Christ, for they are the apple of my eye.

Mr Casey   And can we not love our country then? Are we not to follow the man that was born to lead us?

Dante   A traitor to his country! A traitor, an adulterer! The priests were right to abandon him. The priests were always the true friends of Ireland.

Mr Casey   Were they, faith? Didn't the bishops of Ireland betray us in the time of the Union? Didn't the bishops and priests sell the aspirations of their country in 1829 in return for Catholic emancipation? Didn't they denounce the fenian movement from the pulpit and in the confession box?

Dante   Right! Right! They were always right! God and morality and religion come first.

May   Mrs Riordan, don't excite yourself answering them.

Dante   God and religion before everything! God and religion before the world.

Mr Casey   Very well then, if it comes to that, no God for Ireland!

Simon   John! John!

Mr Casey   No God for Ireland! We have had too much God in Ireland. Away with God!

Dante   Blasphemer! Devil!

Mr Casey   Away with God, I say!

Dante   Devil out of hell! We won! We crushed him to death! Fiend!

Mr Casey (*weeping*)   Poor Parnell! My dead king!

Narrator 1   Stephen, raising his terror-stricken face, saw that his father's eyes were full of tears.

Scene Three

Stephen *is now in class with the Clongowes boys.*

Wells   Who caught them?

Roche   Mr Gleeson and the minister. A fellow in the higher line told me.

Fleming   But why did they run away, tell us?

Roche   Because they had fecked cash out of the rector's room.

Fleming   Who fecked it?

Roche   They all went shares in it.

Fleming   But that was stealing. How could they have done that?

Wells   A fat lot you know about it! I know why they scut.

Roche   Tell us why.

Wells   I was told not to.

Fleming   O, go on, Wells.

Roche   You might tell us.

Stephen 1   We won't let it out.

Wells   You know the altar wine they keep in the press in the sacristy? Well, they drank that and it was found out who did it by the smell. And that's why they ran away, if you want to know.

Roche   Yes, that's what I heard too from the fellow in the higher line.

Athy   You are all wrong.

Fleming   Why? Do you know?

Roche   Who told you?

Athy   I will tell you but you must not let on you know.

Narrator 1   Perhaps they had stolen a monstrance.

Wells   Tell us, Athy. Go on.

Narrator 1   That must have been a terrible sin, to go in there quietly at night, to open the dark press and steal the flashing gold thing into which God was put on the altar. A strange and a great sin even to touch it.

Athy   They were caught with Simon Moonan and Tusker Boyle in the square one night.

Narrator 1   Why in the square? You went there when you wanted to do something. It was all thick slabs of slate and water trickled all day out of tiny pinholes and there was a queer smell of stale water there.

Wells   Caught?

Fleming   What doing?

Athy   Smugging. And that's why.

Fleming   Smugging?

Narrator 1   What did that mean? Why did five fellows out of the higher line run away for that? He wanted to ask somebody. (*Silence.*) Simon Moonan had nice clothes and one night he had shown him a ball of creamy sweets that the fellows of the football fifteen had rolled down to him. And one day Boyle had said that an elephant had two tuskers instead of two tusks and that was why he was called Tusker Boyle but some fellows called him Lady Boyle because he was always at his nails, paring them.

Fleming   What is going to be done to them?

Athy   Simon Moonan and Tusker are going to be flogged, and the fellows in the higher line got their choice of flogging or being expelled.

Wells   And which are they taking?

Athy   All are taking expulsion except Corrigan, He's going to be flogged by Mr Gleeson.

Wells   He is right and the other fellows are wrong. A flogging wears off after a bit but a fellow that has been expelled from college is known all his life on account of it. Besides Gleeson won't flog him hard.

Fleming   It's best of his play not to.

Narrator 1   He remembered how big Corrigan looked in the bath. He had skin the same colour as the turf-coloured bogwater in the shallow end of the bath and when he walked along the side his feet slapped loudly on the wet tiles and at every step his thighs shook a little because he was fat.

Wells   I wouldn't like to be Simon Moonan and Tusker, But I don't believe they will be flogged. Perhaps they will be sent up for twice nine.

Athy   No, no. They'll both get it on the vital spot.

Wells   Please, sir, let me off!

Athy (*sings*)
　　It can't be helped,
　　It must be done,
　　So down with your breeches
　　And out with your bum.

Father Arnall *enters.*

Wells   Sh! Father Arnall!

Father Arnall   Your theme books. All I'll say is, they're a scandal. Scandalous. They're all to be written out again, with the corrections I've marked, do you understand? . . . Do you understand?

Boy   Yes, sir.

Father Arnall   Now, Fleming. Stand. Decline 'mare'.

Fleming   Mare . . . mare . . . maris . . . mari . . . mari . . .

Father Arnall   Yes?

Fleming   Mari . . .

Father Arnall   Mari again? Do you think we might have the plural now?

Fleming (*tentatively trying various words*)   Mar – mar – marum – marium –

Father Arnall   Stop! Kneel there.

Narrator 1   Was that a sin for Father Arnall to be in a wax?

Father Arnall   You are one of the idlest boys I ever met.

Narrator 1   Or was he allowed to get into a wax when the boys were idle?

Father Arnall   You should be ashamed of yourself. Copy out your themes again the rest of you.

Narrator 1   A priest would know what a sin was and would not do it. He had heard his father say that they were all clever men. They could all have become high-up people in the world if they had not become Jesuits. And he wondered what Father Arnall and Mr McGlade would have become if they had not become Jesuits. It was hard to think what because you would have to think of them in a different way with different coloured coats and trousers and with beards and moustaches and different kinds of hats.

Father Dolan *enters.*

Father Dolan   Any boys want flogging here, Father Arnall?

Father Arnall   Father Dolan.

Father Dolan   Any lazy idle loafers that want flogging in this class? Hoho! Who is this boy? Why is he on his knees? What is your name, boy?

Fleming   Fleming, sir.

Father Dolan   Hoho, Fleming! An idler of course. I can see it in your eye. Why is he on his knees, Father Arnall?

Father Arnall   He wrote a bad Latin theme, and he missed all the questions in grammar.

Father Dolan   Of course he did! A born idler! I can see it in the corner of his eye. Up, Fleming! Up, my boy! . . . Hold out! . . . (*Six slaps.*) Other hand! (*Six more.*) Kneel down! At your work, all of you! We want no lazy idle loafers here, lazy idle little schemers. At your work, I tell you. Father Dolan will be in to see you every day. Father Dolan will be in tomorrow. You, boy! When will Father Dolan be in again?

Athy   Tomorrow, sir.

Father Dolan   Tomorrow and tomorrow and tomorrow. Make up your minds for that. Every day Father Dolan.

He makes to exit. After taking a few steps, turns and looks at **Stephen**.

Father Dolan   You, boy, who are you?

Stephen 1   Dedalus, sir.

Father Dolan   Why are you not writing like the others?

Stephen 1   I . . . My . . .

Father Dolan   Why is he not writing, Father Arnall?

Father Arnall   He broke his glasses and I exempted him from work.

Father Dolan   Broke? What is this I hear? What is this your name is!

Stephen 1   Dedalus, sir.

Narrator 1   Was he not listening the first time or was it to make fun out of the name?

Father Dolan   Out here, Dedalus.

Narrator 1   The great men in the history had names like that and nobody made fun of them.

Father Dolan   Lazy little schemer. I see schemer in your face. Where did you break your glasses?

Stephen 1   The cinder path, sir.

Father Dolan   Hoho! The cinder path! I know that trick. Lazy idle little loafer! Broke my glasses! An old schoolboy trick! Out with your hand this moment!

Narrator 1   He felt the touch of the prefect's fingers as they steadied his hand and at first he thought he was going to shake hands with him because the fingers were soft and firm.

The slapping begins.

A hot burning stinging tingling blow like the loud crack of a broken stick made his trembling hand crumple together like a leaf in the fire.

Father Dolan   Other hand!

Six more.

Narrator 1   Was there really something in his face which made him look like a schemer? There could not be; it was unjust and cruel and unfair.

Father Dolan   Kneel down. Get at your work, all of you. Father Dolan will be in every day to see if any boy, any lazy idle little loafer wants flogging. Every day. Every day.

He exits.

Narrator 1   It was unfair and cruel. The doctor had told him not to read without glasses and he had written home to his father that morning to send him a new pair. And Father Arnall had said that he need not study till the new glasses came. It was cruel and unfair to make him kneel in the middle of the class then.

Father Arnall   You may return to your places, you two.

Narrator 1   As if there were no difference between him and Fleming. It was unfair and cruel. The prefect of studies was a priest but that was cruel and unfair.

The class breaks up.

Fleming   It's a stinking mean thing.

Roche   You really broke your glasses by accident, didn't you?

Fleming   Of course he did! I wouldn't stand it. I'd go up and tell the Rector on him.

Roche   Did they hurt you much?

Stephen 1   Very much.

Fleming   I wouldn't stand it. It's a stinking mean low trick, that's what it is. I'd go straight up to the Rector and tell him about it after dinner.

Narrator 1   Yes, he would go up and tell the Rector that he had been wrongly punished.

Roche   Yes, do. Yes, go up and tell the rector on him, Dedalus, because he said that he'd come in tomorrow again and pandy you.

Narrator 1   The Rector would declare that he had been wrongly punished. A thing like that had been done before by somebody in history.

All   Yes, yes. Tell the Rector.

Narrator 1   It was easy what he had to do. Turn to the right and in half a minute he would be in the low dark narrow corridor that led to the Rector's room.

Stephen 1   And every fellow had said that it was unfair.

Narrator 1   But he could not go. The Rector would side with the prefect of studies and think it was a schoolboy trick and then the prefect of studies would come in every day the same.

Stephen 1   Only it would be worse because he would be dreadfully waxy at any fellow going up to the Rector about him.

The boys start to leave the classroom.

Narrator 1   If he went on with the fellows he could never go up to the Rector.

Stephen 1   And if he went and was pandied all the same all the fellows would make fun and talk about young Dedalus going up to tell on the prefect of studies.

Narrator 1   No, it was best to forget all about it and perhaps Father Dolan had only said he would come in.

Stephen 1   It was best to hide out of the way because when you were small and young you could often escape that way.

Narrator 1   Before he could make up his mind to come back, he had entered the low dark narrow corridor.

We see the **Rector**, *sitting in a chair.*

Rector   Come in! . . . Come in! Well, my little man, what is it?

Stephen 1   I broke my glasses, sir.

Rector   O! Well, if we broke our glasses we must write home for a new pair.

Stephen 1   I wrote home, sir, and Father Arnall said I am not to study till they come.

Rector   Quite right!

Stephen 1   But, sir –

Rector   Yes?

Stephen 1   Father Dolan came in today and pandied me because I was not writing my theme.

Rector   Your name is Dedalus, isn't it?

Stephen 1   Yes, sir . . .

Rector   And where did you break your glasses?

Stephen 1   On the cinder path, sir. A fellow was coming out of the bicycle house and I fell and they got broken. I don't know the fellow's name.

Rector   O, well, it was a mistake; I am sure Father Dolan did not know.

Stephen 1   But I told him I broke them, sir, and he pandied me.

Rector   Did you tell him that you had written home for a new pair?

Stephen 1   No, sir.

Rector   O well then, Father Dolan did not understand. You can say that I excuse you from your lessons for a few days.

Stephen 1   Yes, sir, but Father Dolan said he will come in tomorrow to pandy me again for it.

Rector   Very well, it is a mistake and I shall speak to Father Dolan myself. Will that do now?

Stephen 1   O yes, sir, thanks.

Rector   Good day now.

Stephen 1   Good day, sir.

Wells   Three cheers for Dedalus!

The boys cheer.

Narrator 1   The senate and the Roman people declared that Dedalus had been wrongly punished.

Roche   And three groans for Baldyhead Dolan!

Wells   He was alone.

Fleming   He was happy and free.

Stephen 1   The air was soft and grey and mild and evening was coming.

Narrator 1   The fellows were practising long shies and bowling lobs and twisters. In the soft grey silence from here and from there through the quiet air the sound of the cricket bats:

Fleming Pick –

Roche Pack –

Stephen 1 Pock –

Wells Puck –

Narrator 2 Like drops of water in a fountain falling softly in the brimming bowl.

Narrator 1 *now becomes* **Stephen 2**. **Narrator 2** *appears.*

Scene Four

Simon *enters, joining* **May** *and* **Stephen**.

Simon Leave the table in the hall there, we'll find a place to fit everything later. We'll need to get rid of some furniture, it's only getting in the way anyway. (*To* **May**.) What?

May I didn't say anything.

Simon Well, Blackrock will do me, thank you very much. You'll love it being closer to the city, you'll see.

May And a school for Stephen; have you done something about that?

Simon So will you be off adventuring again tomorrow? What's that this young fellow's name is, your friend?

Stephen 2 Aubrey Mills.

Simon Aubrey. You'll be lining up for battle out on the rocks again I suppose?

May It's September. Aubrey is gone back to school. They all are.

Narrator 2 He would not be sent back to Clongowes.

Simon Of course. Aren't you the lucky boy – grand long holiday you're having. What's that you're reading?

Stephen 2   *The Count of Monte Christo.*

Narrator 2   That dark avenger. Outside Blackrock stood a small whitewashed house, in the garden of which grew many rose bushes.

Emma   In this house, he told himself, another Mercedes lived –

Narrator 2   – and in his imagination he lived through a long train of adventures, marvellous as those in the book itself, towards the close of which there appeared an image of himself, grown older and sadder, standing in a moonlit garden with Mercedes who had so many years before slighted his love, and with a sadly proud gesture of refusal, saying:

Stephen 2   Madam, I never eat muscatel grapes.

Narrator 2   As he brooded upon Mercedes' image, a strange unrest crept into his blood.

Emma   Sometimes a fever gathered within him and led him to rove alone in the evening along the quiet avenue.

Narrator 2   The peace of the gardens and the kindly lights in the windows poured a tender influence into his restless heart.

Stephen 2   The noise of children at play annoyed him and their silly voices made him feel, even more keenly than he had felt at Clongowes, that he was different from others.

Narrator 2   He did not want to play.

Emma   He wanted to meet in the real world the unsubstantial image which his soul so constantly beheld.

Narrator 2   And now the family were leaving Blackrock.

Stephen 2   Two great yellow caravans halted one morning before the door and men came tramping into the house.

Narrator 2   The furniture was hustled out through the front garden and when all was safely stowed the vans set off noisily down the avenue, watched by Stephen and his red-eyed mother.

Stephen 2   The sudden flight from the comfort and reverie of Blackrock, the passage through the gloomy foggy city, the thought of the bare cheerless house in which they were to live made his heart heavy.

Simon   I can't get this damn fire to draw.

May   Leave it.

Simon   God knows, it's draughty enough, I can't see why it won't take. Well, they haven't stuck me in the ground yet, not by a long shot. Remember, Stephen, when you set out on life's journey, you'll meet many a two-faced fly-by-night just waiting to put the knife in. Oho, and they'll smile, and tip you the wink, and play the grand fellow – well anyway, they'll get their just desserts, and sooner than they expect. There must be something blocking the flue, is there?

May   I said leave it. Leave it, and find your son a school to go to.

May *exits.* **Simon** *gives up on the fire.*

Simon   There's a crack of the whip left in me yet, Stephen old chap. We're not dead yet, sonny. No, by the Lord Jesus (God forgive me), not half dead.

Stephen *runs to centre stage. Looks around him.*

Wells   Dublin was a new and complex sensation.

Emma   The disorder in settling in the new house, the vastness and strangeness of the life here wakened again the unrest which had sent him wandering in the evening in Blackrock, in search of Mercedes.

Athy   He passed unchallenged among the docks and along the quays wondering at the multitude of corks that lay bobbing on the surface of the water in a thick yellow scum, at the crowds of quay porters and the rumbling carts.

Narrator 2   He might have fancied himself in Marseille but that he missed the bright sky and the sun-warmed trellises of the wine shops. A vague dissatisfaction grew, and yet he continued to wander up and down day after day as if he really sought someone that eluded him.

Scene Five

Stephen *comes face to face with* **Emma***, dressed for a party, putting on her coat.*

Partygoers   Goodbye, Emma. Goodbye!

Emma   Goodbye! Goodbye! Thank you for the lovely party! Stephen . . . are you leaving too?

Stephen 2   Yes.

Emma   Your song was lovely. You have a beautiful voice. Are you getting the tram?

Stephen 2   I . . . yes.

Emma   Come on.

They step on to the tram.

Emma   So you're living in the city now, aren't you?

Stephen *nods.*

Emma   You didn't join in any of the games, did you?

Stephen 2   I suppose I didn't.

Emma   You looked a little gloomy. Weren't you enjoying yourself?

Stephen 2   No, I mean, yes, I was –

Emma   In your own watchful way.

Stephen *laughs.*

Narrator 2   Your heart danced upon her movements like a cork upon a tide. You hear what her eyes say to you from beneath their cowl. In some time past, you have heard their tale before. Will you take her gift? You only have to stretch out your hand.

Stephen 2   She too wants me to catch hold of her. That's why she came with me on the tram. I could easily catch hold of her when she comes up to my step: nobody is looking. I could hold her and kiss her.

Emma   Here we are. Bye, Stephen.

Stephen 2   Bye.

Narrator 2   But you did neither.

Stephen *tears up his ticket slowly, then runs and fetches a pen and notebook, and goes to the table to write.*

Stephen 2
   To E, dash, C, dash.
   The conductor talked with the driver . . .

He isn't happy with this.

   The green light of the lamp . . .

Not quite right either.

   The lank brown horses shook their bells . . .

He shakes his head, scribbles out a line, then a flash of inspiration.

Stephen 2
   The balmy breeze . . .

He nods to himself. Cracked it. Writes furiously. Pauses.

   The maiden lustre of the moon . . .

He's impressed with this, and keeps writing.

   With secret sorrows hidden in each heart –

Narrator 2
   And at the moment of farewell –

Stephen 2/Narrator 2
That kiss was granted, which she had withheld.

He's satisfied. Lights go down slowly.

Scene Six

Lights up on **Stephen**, **Simon** *and* **May** *at the dinner table.*

Simon   I walked bang into him, just at the corner of the square!

May   Then I suppose he'll be able to arrange it? I mean about sending Stephen to Belvedere.

May *furtively looks toward* **Stephen**, *not sure if he should be hearing this.*

Simon   Of course he will. Don't I tell you he's provincial of the order now?

May   I never liked the idea of sending him to the Christian Brothers myself.

Simon   Christian Brothers be damned! Is it with Paddy Stink and Micky Mud? No, let him stick to the Jesuits in God's name since he began with them. They'll be of service to him in after years. Those are the fellows that can get you a position.

May   And they're a very rich order, aren't they, Simon?

Simon   Rather. They live well, I tell you. You saw their table at Clongowes. Fed up, by God, like gamecocks. Now then, Stephen, you must put your shoulder to the wheel, old chap. You've had a fine long holiday.

May   O, I'm sure he'll work very hard now.

Simon   By the bye, the Rector, or Provincial rather, was telling me that story about you and Father Dolan. You're an impudent thief, he said.

May   O, he didn't, Simon!

Simon   Not he! But he gave me a great account of the whole affair. We were chatting, you know, and one word borrowed another. And, by the way, who do you think he told me will get that job in the corporation? But I'll tell you that after. Well, we were chatting away and he asked me did our friend here wear glasses still, and then he told me the whole story.

May   And was he annoyed, Simon?

Simon   Annoyed? Not he! Manly little chap! he said. (*In Rector's voice.*) 'Father Dolan and I, when I told them all at dinner about it, Father Dolan and I had a great laugh over it. You better mind yourself, Father Dolan, said I, or young Dedalus will send you up for twice nine! We had a famous laugh together over it. Ha! Ha! Ha!' (*Normal voice.*) Shows you the spirit in which they take the boys there. O, a Jesuit for your life, for diplomacy! (*Rector voice.*) 'I told them all at dinner about it and Father Dolan and I and all of us we had a hearty laugh together over it. Ha! Ha! Ha!'

Scene Seven

Stephen *gathers up his schoolbooks and walks over to the desks, where other boys join him. A teacher,* **Mr Tate***, starts handing out marked essays.* **Mr Tate** *comes to* **Stephen***. Holds up his essay.*

Mr Tate   Now since young Dedalus joined this class, he's turned in some first-rate essays. Top of the class more often than not, would I be right?

Stephen 2   Yes, Mr Tate.

Mr Tate   But today, this fellow has heresy in his essay. Perhaps you didn't know that.

Stephen 2   Where?

Mr Tate   Here. It's about the Creator and the soul. Rrm . . .
rrm . . . rrm . . . Ah! 'Without a possibility of ever
approaching nearer.' That's heresy.

Stephen 2   I meant without a possibility of ever reaching.

Mr Tate   O . . . Ah! Ever reaching. That's another story.

With an indulgent chuckle, **Mr Tate** *pats him on the shoulder, and
exits.*

Heron   Who is the greatest writer, Dedalus?

Stephen 2   Of prose do you mean?

Heron   Yes.

Stephen 2   Newman, I think.

Boland   Is it Cardinal Newman?

Stephen 2   Yes.

Heron   O, many say that Newman has the best prose style,
of course he's not a poet.

Boland   And who is the best poet, Heron?

Heron   Lord Tennyson, of course, Boland.

Boland   O, yes, Lord Tennyson. We have all his poetry at
home in a book.

Stephen 2   Tennyson, he's only a rhymester!

Heron   O, get out! Everyone knows that Tennyson is the
greatest poet.

Boland   And who do you think is the greatest poet?

Stephen 2   Byron, of course.

The others laugh.

Heron   Byron's only a poet for uneducated people.

Stephen 2   You may keep your mouth shut.

Heron   Byron was a heretic and immoral too.

Stephen 2   I don't care what he was.

Heron   You don't care whether he was a heretic or not?

Stephen 2   What do you know about it? You never read a line of anything in your life except a translation, or Boland either.

Boland   I know that Byron was a bad man.

Heron   Tate made you buck up there, about the heresy in your essay.

Boland   Why are you always moving house, Dedalus?

Heron   Why did you leave Clongowes?

Boland   You're a free boy, aren't you?

Heron   Admit that Byron was no good. Here, catch hold of this heretic.

Heron *and* **Boland** *both grab* **Stephen** *and hit him.*

Boland   Admit.

Stephen 2   No.

Heron   Admit.

Stephen 2   No.

Boland   Admit.

Stephen 2   No. No.

Scene Eight

A boy enters, calls **Stephen**.

Boy   Dedalus! The audience are coming in. Mr Tate is showing them to their seats. You're on soon, Dedalus.

Stephen 2   Not for ages yet.

Priest Is this a beautiful young lady or a doll that we have here? No! Upon my word I believe it's little Bertie Tallon after all! On you go my pretty!

Heron I saw your governor going in. You're a sly dog.

Stephen 2 Why so?

Heron You'd think butter wouldn't melt in your mouth.

Stephen 2 Might I ask you what you are talking about?

Heron Indeed you might. We saw her. And deucedly pretty she is too. And inquisitive! And what part does Stephen take, Mr Dedalus? And will Stephen not sing, Mr Dedalus? Your governor was staring at her through that eyeglass of his for all he was worth, so I think the old man has found you out too. You can't play the saint on me any more! You're on the lookout for her now, aren't you?

He smacks **Stephen** *playfully with his cane.*

Heron Admit!

Smacking him again, harder.

Stephen 2 *Confiteor Deo omnipotenti, beatae Mariae semper Virgini . . .*

They laugh. A boy runs up.

Boy O, Dedalus, Tate is in a great bake about you. Hurry up, you better.

Heron He's coming now, when he wants to.

Boy But Tate is in an awful bake.

Heron Will you tell Tate with my best compliments that I damned his eyes?

Stephen 2 I must go now.

Heron I wouldn't, damn me if I would. I think it's quite enough that you're taking a part in his bally old play.

Stephen *dons a clownish pedagogue's costume.*

Mr Tate   Now speak up, remember? The diction. The breathing. Make your points clearly.

Boland   Look at Dedalus!

Boy   You're on next, Stephen!

Boland   Good luck, Stephen!

Heron   Break a leg!

Narrator 2   The excitement about him entered into and transformed his moody mistrustfulness, and for one rare moment he seemed to be clothed in the real apparel of boyhood.

Stephen *walks slowly to the front of the stage, accompanied by the* **Narrator**.

Narrator 2   She would be sitting there among the others. He tried to recall her appearance but could remember only that she had worn a shawl about her head and that her dark eyes had invited and unnerved him.

Emma   Had he been in her thoughts as she had been in his?

Narrator 2   Her serious alluring eyes watching from among the audience. Another nature seemed to have been lent him: The play suddenly assumed a life of its own. It seemed now to play itself; he and his fellow actors aiding it with their parts.

Stephen *bows, turns.*

Narrator 2   Now his nerves cried for some further adventure. He hurried onwards as if to overtake it.

May   That was marvellous Stephen!

Simon   What did I tell you? A chip off the old block!

May   You had it to a 't', now, really.

Stephen 2   Thanks . . . eh . . .

He looks over their shoulders. Where's **Emma**?

Simon   Did I detect the distinctive mannerisms of a certain rector there by any chance?

May   O, Stephen you didn't! Will that be alright, though?

Simon   Yerra, of course. They wouldn't mind that.

May   Are you missing something, love?

Stephen 2   I have to leave a message down in George's Street. I'll be home after you.

He pushes past them.

Simon   What? But Stephen –

Narrator 2   He ran across the road and began to walk at breakneck speed –

Stephen 2   Down the hill –

Narrator 2   He hardly knew where he was walking.

Stephen 2   Down –

Narrator 2   Pride and hope and desire like crushed herbs in his heart sent up vapours of maddening incense before the eyes of his mind.

Stephen 2   Down the hill –

Narrator 2   He strode amid the tumult of sudden-risen vapours of wounded pride and fallen hope and baffled desire. They streamed upwards before his anguished eyes in dense and maddening fumes –

Stephen *slows down.*

Narrator 2   And passed away above him till at last the air was clear and cold again.

A film still veiled his eyes but they burned no longer.

He stood still and gazed up at the sombre porch of the morgue.

And from that to the dark cobbled laneway at its side. He breathed slowly the rank heavy air.

Stephen 2   That is horse piss and rotted straw. It is a good odour to breathe. It will calm my heart. My heart is quite calm now. I will go back.

As he turns, the lights change.

Narrator 2 *now becomes* **Stephen 3**. **Narrator 3** *appears.*

Scene Nine

Simon (*sings*)
      'Tis youth and folly
      Makes young men marry,
      So here, my love,
      I'll no longer stay.
      What can't be cured, sure,
      Must be endured, sure,
      So I'll go to Amerikay.

Narrator 3   The bright warm sunlight was streaming through the window of the Victoria Hotel, Cork. His father's property was going to be sold by auction.

Simon
      My love she's handsome,
      My love she's bonny:
      She's like good whisky
      When it is new;
      But when 'tis old
      And growing cold
      It fades and dies like
      The mountain dew.

Stephen 3   That's much prettier than any of your other come-all-yous.

Simon   Do you think so?

Stephen 3   I like it.

He begins to help his father with his collar, studs, tie, etc.

Simon   It's a pretty old air. Ah, but you should have heard Mick Lacy sing it! Poor Mick Lacy! He had little turns for it, grace notes that he used to put in that I haven't got. That was the boy who could sing a come-all-you, if you like. Did you like your drisheen?

They both laugh.

Narrator 3   At breakfast, Mr Dedalus's cup had rattled noisily against its saucer, and Stephen had tried to cover that shameful sign of his father's drinking bout of the night before by moving his chair and coughing.

Simon   A good Cork breakfast. God I thought I'd lost my reason talking to that poor waiter though. Or that he had. I asked after Con Sweeney and says he, oh, Con's never been better. Great man for the football. The football? Of course he was talking about Con the son. Or grandson actually, probably. Well, in the end I said to him, I hope they haven't moved the Queen's College anyhow!

A **Porter** *appears.*

Porter   Through here, sir, feel free to look around −

Simon   I want to show it to this youngster of mine. Now if they still have the same desks it should be in here −

Narrator 3   Into the anatomy theatre where Mr Dedalus searched the desks for his initials.

Simon   Ah, do you tell me so? And is poor Pottlebelly dead?

Porter   Yes, sir. Ah, years ago now, sir.

Narrator 3   On the desk, the word 'Foetus', cut several times in the dark stained wood. The sudden legend startled his blood. He seemed to feel the absent students of the college about. A vision of their life sprang up before him out of the word cut in the desk.

Simon   Ah! Here we are! Stephen! Still there, you see? S.D., look?

Narrator 3 'Foetus'. The word and the vision capered before his eyes. Monstrous reveries came thronging. He had allowed them to sweep across and abase his intellect, restless and sickened of himself.

Simon A crowd of us, Harry Peard and little Jack Mountain and Bob Dyas.

Narrator 3 He heard again the names of the scattered and dead revellers who had been the companions of his father's youth.

Simon Maurice Moriarty, the Frenchman, and Tom Grady –

Narrator 3 A faint sickness sighed in his heart. He recalled his own equivocal position in Belvedere –

Stephen 3 A free boy –

Narrator 3 Proud and sensitive and suspicious, battling against the squalor of his life and against the riot of his mind.

Simon And Mick Lacy that I told you of this morning and poor little good-hearted Johnny Keevers of the Tantiles.

Narrator 3 The letters cut in the stained wood of the desk stared upon him, mocking his bodily weakness and futile enthusiasms.

Stephen 3 I am Stephen Dedalus. I am walking beside my father whose name is Simon Dedalus. We are in Cork, in Ireland. Cork is a city. Our room is in the Victoria Hotel.

Narrator 3 Victoria and Stephen and Simon. Simon and Stephen and Victoria. Names.

Simon When I was a young fellow, Stephen, I mixed with fine decent fellows. One fellow had a good voice, another fellow was a good actor, another could sing a good comic song, another was a good oarsman and so on. We kept the ball rolling anyhow and enjoyed ourselves and saw a bit of life and we were none the worse of it either. But we were all gentlemen, Stephen, and bloody good honest Irishmen too.

That's the kind of fellows I want you to associate with, fellows
of the right kidney. I'm talking to you as a friend, Stephen, I
treat you as your grandfather treated me when I was a young
chap. We were more like brothers than father and son. I'll
never forget the first day he caught me smoking. I was
standing at the end of the South Terrace one day with some
maneens like myself and sure we thought we were grand
fellows because we had pipes stuck in the corners of our
mouths. Suddenly the governor passed. He didn't say a word,
or stop even. But the next day we were out for a walk together
and when we were coming home he took out his cigar case
and said – 'By the bye, Simon, I didn't know you smoked,'
or something like that. 'If you want a good smoke, try one
of these cigars.' He was the handsomest man in Cork at that
time, by God he was! The women used to stand to look after
him in the street.

Simon *laughs / sobs. He and* **Stephen** *stand and watch as an
auctioneer begins the sale.*

Auctioneer   From the same consignment, property of
an old Cork family, wardrobe and chest of drawers, fair
condition, starting the bidding at six shillings, six shillings,
now, six, do I hear six, anyone, six shillings, five shillings
anyone prepared to bid five, five shillings do I hear five and
sixpence any advance on five, still five, going for five, last bids
now please, going for five, still five, going, going –

Simon   Come on, in God's name we'll come back when
they've picked us clean, Stephen.

Narrator 3   Stephen followed his father meekly about the
city from bar to bar. One humiliation succeeded another –

Athy   The false smiles of the market sellers –

Stephen 3   The curvetings and oglings of the barmaids
with whom his father flirted –

Wells   The compliments and encouraging words of his
father's friends.

Barman   He has a look of his grandfather about him.

Simon, *very drunk, is holding court.*

Simon   Arrah, there's an ugly likeness, sure enough. I'm an old Corkonian, and that Peter Pickackafax beside me is my eldest son but he's only a Dublin jackeen. Not half my age and I'm a better man than he is any day of the week.

Barman   Draw it mild now, Dedalus, it's time for you to take a back seat.

Simon   No, by God! I'll sing a tenor song against him or I'll vault a five-barred gate against him or I'll run with him after the hounds across the country as I did thirty years ago along with the Kerry Boy and the best man for it.

Barman (*tapping his forehead*)   But he'll beat you here.

Simon   Well, I hope he'll be as good a man as his father. That's all I can say.

Barman   If he is, he'll do.

Simon   And thanks be to God, Johnny, that we lived so long and did so little harm.

Barman   But did so much good, Simon. Thanks be to God we lived so long and did so much good.

Narrator 3   Stephen watched the glasses being raised from the counter as his father and his cronies drank to the memory of their past.

An abyss of fortune or of temperament sundered him from them. His mind seemed older than theirs: it shone coldly on their strifes and happiness and regrets like a moon upon a younger earth. No life or youth stirred in him as it had stirred in them. He had known neither the pleasure of companionship with others nor the vigour of rude male health nor filial piety. Nothing stirred within his soul but a cold and cruel and loveless lust. His childhood was dead or lost and with it his soul capable of simple joys and he was drifting amid life like the barren shell of the moon.

Scene Ten

Mr Tate *is standing at the benches.*

Mr Tate   Dedalus!

Stephen 3   Mr Tate?

Mr Tate   I wanted to talk to you about that essay.

Stephen 3   Which essay, sir?

Mr Tate   The one you submitted for the national prize.

Stephen 3   Yes sir?

Mr Tate   Did you manage to keep it free of heresy?

Stephen 3   I think so, sir.

Mr Tate   You must have. Or if there was heresy the adjudicators missed it.

Stephen 3   Sir?

Mr Tate   First prize. A cheque for thirty pounds. Very well done.

Stephen 3   Thank you, sir.

He raises the cheque in triumph.

Narrator 3   For a swift season of merrymaking the money of his prizes ran through Stephen's fingers.

The family gather round.

Stephen 3   We had better go to dinner.

Simon   Dinner? Well, I suppose we had better, what?

May   Some place that's not too dear.

Simon   Yes. Some quiet place.

Stephen 3   Come along. It doesn't matter about the dearness.

Narrator 3   Great parcels of groceries and delicacies and dried fruits arrived from the city. He bought presents for everyone, overhauled his room, wrote out resolutions, marshalled his books up and down their shelves, and opened a loan bank for his family so that he might have the pleasure of making out receipts and reckoning the interests on the sums lent.

May   O Stephen, it's lovely, you shouldn't have!

Stephen 3   That comes due at the end of the month and no later.

Maurice   Plus two and a half per cent, I'll have it, don't worry.

Narrator 3   Every day he drew up a bill of fare for the family and every night led a party of three or four to the theatre to see *Ingomar* or *The Lady of Lyons*. In his coat pockets he carried squares of Vienna chocolate for his guests while his trousers' pocket bulged with masses of silver and copper coins.

Simon   Stephen?

Stephen 3   What?

Simon   Stephen?

Stephen 3   Oh.

He hands **Simon** *some money.*

Simon   A true gentleman. Can I get you a jar?

Stephen 3   No, but while you're down that way can you buy a bit of beef for tomorrow?

Simon   Beef is it? O, of course. Of course.

Stephen 3   Put those books over there, Maurice, I'll stack them myself.

Maurice   Are you going to the theatre again tonight?

Stephen 3   We're all going.

Narrator 3   Then the season of pleasure came to an end. His household returned to its usual way of life.

Maurice   The loan bank closed its books on a sensible loss.

Narrator 3   And the rules of life which he had drawn about himself fell into desuetude.

Stephen 3   How foolish I had been!

Narrator 3   He had tried to build a breakwater of order and elegance against the sordid tide of life. Useless. He saw clearly his own futile isolation. He had not gone one step nearer the lives he had sought to approach.

Stephen 3   His blood was in revolt. He returned to his wanderings, searching now up and down the dark slimy streets like some baffled prowling beast.

He walks away. In the darkness, he passes by a girl, then another. Sounds of bar music, bottles breaking in the street.

Girl 1   Goodnight, husband! Coming in for a short time?

Narrator 3   Women and girls in long vivid gowns traversed the street, leisurely and perfumed.

Girl 4   Is that you, pigeon?

Narrator 3   He was in another world: he had awakened from a slumber of centuries.

Girl 3   Fresh Nellie is waiting for you.

Narrator 3   He wanted to sin with another of his kind, to force another being to sin and to exult with her in sin.

A girl approaches, puts her hand on **Stephen***'s arm.*

Girl 2   Goodnight, Willie dear!

Narrator 3   Her room was warm and lightsome. He tried to bid his tongue speak that he might seem at ease.

Girl 2   It's alright. Come here.

The girl embraces **Stephen***.*

Narrator 3   His lips parted, though he could not speak.

Girl 2   Ah. You little rascal. Give me a kiss.

Narrator 3   His lips would not bend to kiss her. He wanted to be held firmly in her arms, to be caressed slowly, slowly, slowly. But his lips would not bend to kiss her.

Girl 2   Gimme a kiss.

Narrator 3   With a sudden movement she bowed his head and joined her lips to his and he read the meaning of her movements in her frank uplifted eyes.

It was too much for him. He closed his eyes, surrendering himself to her, body and mind, conscious of nothing in the world but the dark pressure of her softly parting lips.

They pressed upon his brain as upon his lips as though they were the vehicle of a vague speech; and between them he felt an unknown and timid pressure, darker than the swoon of sin, softer than sound or odour.

Scene Eleven

Lights up on the benches, where **Stephen 3** *is now sitting, with other students.*

Mr Tate   Well now, Ennis, I declare you have a head and so has my stick! Do you mean to say that you are not able to tell me what a surd is?

Ennis   A surd, sir?

Girl 2 *from the previous scene comes and drapes herself over* **Stephen**, *unseen to anyone but him.*

Mr Tate   Ye–es, a surd, go on.

Girl 3   Fresh Nelly is waiting on you!

Girl 1   Coming in to have a short time?

Narrator 3   There would be stew for dinner, turnips and carrots and bruised potatoes and fat mutton pieces to be ladled out in thick peppered flour-fattened sauce. Stuff it into you, his belly counselled him.

Girl 4 (*continues under narration*)   Stuff it into you . . .

Girl 3   Stuff it into you . . .

Girl 2   Stuff it . . . into you . . .

Girl 1 (*continues under narration*)   Stuff it . . . into you . . .

Narrator 3   He had sinned mortally not once but many times and he knew that, while he stood in danger of eternal damnation for the first sin alone, by every succeeding sin he multiplied his guilt and his punishment.

Girl 2   Stuff it . . . into you.

Ennis   It's . . . a . . . a number . . .

Girl 1   Stuff it . . . into you.

Mr Tate   Go on, boy.

Girl 3   Stuff it . . . into you.

Narrator 3   Strangely, this sin, which had covered him from the sight of God, had led him nearer to Mary, the refuge of sinners. Her eyes seemed to regard him with mild pity; her holiness, a strange light glowing faintly upon her frail flesh.

Girl 4   Stuff it . . . into you.

Girl 2   Her emblem is the morning star. Bright and musical, telling of Heaven –

Ennis   It isn't . . .

Girl 2   A prefect of the Sodality of the Blessed Virgin –

Ennis   It isn't . . . rational?

Mr Tate   Look over it, look over it. The retreat will begin on Wednesday afternoon in honour of Saint Francis Xavier, whose feast day is Saturday.

Father Arnall *appears*

Stephen 3   Father Arnall!

Narrator 3   The figure of his old master, so strangely re-arisen, brought back to Stephen's mind his life at Clongowes: the wide playgrounds, the square ditch; the firelight on the wall of the infirmary where he lay sick. His soul, as these memories came back to him, became again a child's soul.

Father Arnall   Help me, my dear little brothers in Christ. Help me by your pious attention. Banish from your minds all worldly thoughts and think only of the last things: death, judgement, hell, and heaven.

Narrator 3   The faint glimmer of fear became a terror of spirit as Father Arnall blew death into Stephen's soul.

Father Arnall   One single instant is enough for the trial of a man's soul. One single instant after the body's death, the soul will be weighed in the balance, / and will pass to the abode of bliss or to the prison of purgatory or be hurled howling into hell.

Narrator 3   Every word of it was for him. Against his sin, foul and secret, the whole wrath of God was aimed. The wind of the last day blew through his mind; and his sins, / the jewel-eyed harlots of his imagination, fled before the hurricane, squeaking like mice in their terror.

Father Arnall   Hell is a dark and foul-smelling prison, an abode of demons and lost souls, filled with fire and smoke. By reason of the great number of the damned, the prisoners are heaped together, so utterly bound and helpless that they are not even able to remove from the eye a worm that gnaws it.

Narrator 3   The walls of hell are said to be / four thousand miles thick.

Father Arnall   It is a never-ending storm of darkness, dark flames and dark smoke of burning brimstone, amid which the bodies are heaped one upon another without even a glimpse of air –

Narrator 3 – some foul and putrid corpse that has lain rotting and decomposing in the grave, a jelly-like mass of liquid / corruption.

Father Arnall These devils, they mock and jeer at the lost souls whom they dragged down to ruin. It is they, the foul demons, who are made in hell the voices of conscience.

Narrator 3 Why did you sin?

Father Arnall Why did you turn aside from your pious practices and good works?

Narrator 3 Why did you not shun the occasions of sin?

Father Arnall Why did you not leave that evil companion?

The prostitute **Girl 2** *appears, and whispers to* **Stephen**.

Girl 2 Why did you not give up that lewd habit, that impure habit?

Father Arnall Why did you not listen to the counsels of your confessor?

Narrator 3 Why did you not repent of your evil ways and turn to God who only waited for your repentance to absolve you of your sins?

Girl 2 Absolve you of your sins.

Father Arnall Now the time for repentance has gone by. Time is, time was, but time shall be no more!

Girl 2 Time was to sin in secrecy, to covet the unlawful, to yield to the promptings of your lower nature.

Father Arnall To live like the beasts of the field.

Girl 2 Stuff it into you.

Father Arnall Such is the language of those fiendish tormentors, words of taunting and of reproach, of hatred and of disgust. Of disgust, yes! For even they, the very devils, must turn away, revolted and disgusted, from the contemplation of those unspeakable sins by which degraded man outrages and defiles the temple of the Holy Ghost –

Girl 2/Narrator 3   Defiles and pollutes himself.

Narrator 3   Shame rose from his smitten heart and flooded his whole being. The image of Emma appeared before him, and under her eyes the flood of shame rushed forth anew from his heart. If she knew to what his mind had subjected her or how his brute-like lust had torn and trampled upon her innocence! Was that boyish love? Was that chivalry? Was that poetry? Mad! Mad! Was it possible he had done these things? A cold sweat broke out upon his forehead as the foul memories condensed within his brain.

Father Arnall   *Non serviam:* I will not serve; the sinful thought of one instant for which God cast Lucifer into hell for ever. Place your finger for a moment in the flame of a candle and you will feel the pain of fire. The sulphurous brimstone in hell is specially designed to burn for ever and for ever /with unspeakable fury.

Some Boys (*whisper*)   Oh my God . . . Oh my God . . .

Father Arnall   I pray fervently that not a single soul of those who are in this chapel today may be found among those miserable beings, that not one of us may ever hear ringing in his ears the awful sentence of rejection: Depart from me ye cursed, into everlasting fire which was prepared for the devil and his angels!

O my God! –

All   – O my God! –

Father Arnall   I am heartily sorry –

All   – I am heartily sorry –

Father Arnall   – for having offended Thee –

All   – for having offended Thee –

Father Arnall   – and I detest my sins –

All   – and I detest my sins –

Father Arnall   – above every other evil –

All   – above every other evil –

Father Arnall   – because they displease Thee, my God –

All   – because they displease Thee, my God –

Father Arnall   – Who art so deserving –

All   – Who art so deserving –

Father Arnall   – of all my love –

All   – of all my love –

Father Arnall   – and I firmly purpose –

All   – and I firmly purpose –

Father Arnall   – by Thy holy grace –

All   – by Thy holy grace –

Father Arnall   – never more to offend Thee –

All   – never more to offend Thee –

Father Arnall   – and to amend my life –

All   – and to amend my life –

Father Arnall   Amen.

All   Amen.

Narrator 3   One soul was lost; a tiny soul: his. It flickered once and went out, forgotten, lost. The end: black, cold, void waste.

Narrator 3 *now becomes* **Stephen 4**. **Narrator 4** *appears*.

Stephen *accosts an* **Old Woman**.

Stephen 4   Is there a chapel near here?

Old Woman   A chapel, sir? Yes, sir. Church Street chapel.

Stephen 4   Church? (*She points the way.*) Thank you. Thank you.

Old Woman   You are quite welcome, sir.

Stephen *kneels. We hear a priest's voice.*

Simon   How long is it since your last confession, my child?

Stephen 4   A long time, Father.

Dante   A month, my child?

Stephen 4   Longer, Father.

Stephen 2   Three months, my child?

Stephen 4   Longer, Father.

Athy   Six months?

Stephen 4   Eight months, Father.

Stephen 1   And what do you remember since that time?

Stephen 4   I . . . I missed Mass, Father. I neglected my prayers. And . . .

Emma   Yes, my child?

Stephen 4   I told lies, Father . . .

Dolan   Anything else, my child?

Stephen 4   I committed the sin of anger, I envied others, I . . . I was gluttonous. I disobeyed my teachers, I disobeyed my parents . . .

May   And was there anything else, my child?

Stephen 4   I . . . committed sins of impurity, Father.

Priest   . . . With yourself, my child?

Stephen 4   And . . . with others.

Priest   With women, my child?

Stephen 4   Yes, Father.

Priest   Were they married women, my child?

Stephen 4   He did not know. His sins trickled from his lips, one by one, trickled in shameful drops from his soul, festering and oozing like a sore, a squalid stream of vice. The last sins oozed forth, sluggish, filthy. There was no more to tell.

Long pause.

Priest   How old are you, my child?

Stephen 4   Sixteen, Father.

Priest   You are very young, my child, and let me implore of you to give up that sin. It is a terrible sin. It kills the body and it kills the soul. It is the cause of many crimes and misfortunes. Give it up, my child, for God's sake. Pray to Our Blessed Lady when that sin comes into your mind. I am sure you will do that, will you not? You repent of all those sins. I am sure you do. And you will promise God now that by His holy grace you will never offend Him any more by that wicked sin. You will make that solemn promise to God, will you not?

Stephen 4   Yes, Father.

Priest   *Dominus noster Jesus Christus te absolvat; / et ego auctoritate ipsius te absolvo ab omni vinculo excommunicationis et interdicti in quantum possum et tu indiges. Deinde, ego te absolvo a peccatis tuis in nomine Patris, et Filii, et Spiritus Sancti.* Amen.

Narrator 4 *(over prayer)*   How simple and beautiful was life after all! His prayers ascended to Heaven from his purified heart like perfume streaming upwards from a heart of white rose. Holy and happy. It would be beautiful to die if God so willed. It was beautiful to live a life of grace and virtue and happiness! Another life! It was not a dream. The past was past!

Priest   God bless you my child. Pray for me.

Narrator 4 *and* **Stephen 4**   The past was past!

Interval.

Act Two

Scene One

Stephen *alternately kneels, walks to another part of the stage, then kneels again, always in fervent prayer.*

Narrator 4   Sunday was dedicated to –

Stephen 4   – the mystery of the Holy Trinity.

Narrator 4   Monday –

Stephen 4   – the Holy Ghost.

Narrator 4   Tuesday –

Stephen 4   – the guardian angels.

Narrator 4   Wednesday –

Stephen 4   – Saint Joseph.

Narrator 4   Thursday –

Stephen 4   – the most Blessed Sacrament of the Altar.

Narrator 4   Friday –

Stephen 4   – the Suffering Jesus.

Narrator 4   Saturday –

Stephen 4   – the Blessed Virgin Mary.

Narrator 4   His daily life was laid out in devotional areas. Every thought, word, and deed, every instance of consciousness could be made to re-vibrate radiantly in Heaven.

Stephen *adopts a kneeling position, arms upraised.*

Stephen 4   Hail Mary full of grace, the Lord is with thee –

Narrator 4   On each of the seven days of the week he further prayed that one of the seven gifts of the Holy Ghost might descend upon him.

Stephen 4   Holy Mary, Mother of God –

Narrator 4   Gradually, he saw the whole world forming one vast symmetrical expression of God's power and love. So entire was this sense of the divine meaning that he could scarcely understand why it was necessary that he should continue to live.

Stephen 4   O my God, I am heartily sorry –

Narrator 4   Yet that was part of the divine purpose and he dared not question its use, he above all others who had sinned so deeply and so foully against the divine purpose.

Stephen 4   I firmly resolve, with the help of Thy grace, to confess my sins, to do penance, and to amend my life. Amen.

Narrator 4   He strove by constant mortification to undo the sinful past. Each of his senses was brought under a rigorous discipline, but it was to the mortification of touch he brought the most assiduous ingenuity of inventiveness. He suffered patiently every itch and pain, remained on his knees all through the Mass, left part of his neck and face undried so that air might sting them and, whenever he was not saying his beads, carried his arms stiffly at his sides like a runner and never in his pockets or clasped behind him. He had no temptations to sin mortally. It surprised him however to find he was still so easily at the mercy of childish and unworthy imperfections. His prayers and fasts availed him little for the suppression of anger at being disturbed in his devotions –

May *sneezes.* **Stephen** *closes his eyes and clenches his fists.*

Narrator 4   – and a restless feeling of guilt would always be present with him: perhaps that first hasty confession wrung from him by the fear of hell had not been good? But the surest sign that his confession had been good was, he knew, the amendment of his life.

Stephen 4   I have amended my life, have I not?

Scene Two

The **Director of Studies** *enters, indicates to* **Stephen** *to sit at the table.*

Director   Sit down, sit down. What was I saying?

Stephen 4   The capuchin dress . . .

Narrator 4   Ever since the summons had come from the Father Director, Stephen's mind had struggled to find the meaning of the message.

Director   Ah, yes! The capuchin dress, I think, is rather too, eh . . . I believe there is some talk now among the capuchins themselves of doing away with it.

Stephen 4   I suppose they would retain it in the cloisters?

Director   O certainly, but for the street I really think it would be better to do away with it, don't you?

Stephen 4   It must be troublesome, I imagine.

Director   Of course it is, of course. Just imagine when I was in Belgium I used to see them out cycling in all kinds of weather with this thing up about their knees! It was really ridiculous. *Les jupes*, they call them in Belgium.

Stephen 4   What do they call them?

Director   *Les jupes*. Skirts . . . I sent for you today, Stephen, because I wished to speak to you on a very important subject.

Stephen 4   Yes, sir.

Director   Have you ever felt that you had a vocation? I mean, have you ever felt within yourself, in your soul, a desire to join the order? Think.

Stephen 4   I have sometimes thought of it.

Director   In a college like this, there is one boy or perhaps two or three boys whom God calls to the religious life. Perhaps you are the boy in this college. To receive that call,

Stephen, is the greatest honour that the Almighty God can bestow upon a man.

Narrator 4   How often had he seen himself as a priest wielding calmly and humbly the awful power of which angels and saints stood in reverence! His soul had loved to muse in secret on this desire.

Director   No king or emperor on this earth has the power of the priest of God. No angel or archangel in heaven, no saint, not even the Blessed Virgin herself, has the power of a priest of God: the power of the keys, the power to bind and to loose from sin, the power of exorcism, the power to cast out from the creatures of God the evil spirits that have power over them; the power, the authority, to make the great God of Heaven come down upon the altar and take the form of bread and wine. I will offer up my Mass tomorrow morning, that Almighty God may reveal to you His holy will. And let you, Stephen, make a novena to your holy patron saint, the first martyr, who is very powerful with God, that God may enlighten your mind. But you must be quite sure, Stephen, that you have a vocation because it would be terrible if you found afterwards that you had none. Once a priest always a priest, remember. It is before you must weigh well, not after. It is a solemn question, Stephen, because on it may depend the salvation of your eternal soul.

Narrator 4   A grave and ordered and passionless life awaited, a life without material cares. He wondered how he would pass the first night in the novitiate and with what dismay he would wake the first morning in the dormitory. The troubling odour of the long corridors of Clongowes came back to him.

Emma   Passing before the Jesuit house in Gardiner Street he wondered vaguely which window would be his if he joined the order.

Narrator 4   Then he wondered at the vagueness of his wonder.

Various voices, overlapping, a growing cacophony:

Wells   O, I say, here's a fellow says he kisses his mother every night before he goes to bed.

Athy   Do you see the joke? Athy is the town in the County Kildare and a thigh is the other thigh.

Dante   . . . and the brush with the green velvet back is for Parnell.

Mr Casey   Poor Parnell! My dead king!

Stephen 4   You really broke your glasses by accident, didn't you?

May   It's September. Aubrey is gone back to school. They all are.

Emma   You have a beautiful voice. Are you getting the tram?

Simon   Is it with Paddy Stink and Micky Mud?

Heron   Who is the greatest writer, Dedalus?

Boy   Mr Tate is showing them to their seats. You're on soon, Dedalus.

Nellie   Fresh Nellie is waiting on you.

Father Arnall   *Non serviam.*

Narrator 4   *Non serviam.* The wisdom of the Director's appeal did not touch you to the quick. You were destined to learn your own wisdom wandering among the snares of the world. The snares of the world were its ways of sin. You will fall. You have not yet fallen but you will fall silently, in an instant. Not to fall is too hard, too hard.

Stephen 4 *and* **Narrator 4**   *Non serviam.*

Narrator 4   On the lane up to his house, the faint sour stink of rotted cabbages came towards him from the kitchen gardens on the rising ground above the river.

Director This disorder, the misrule and confusion of his father's house and the stagnation of vegetable life, this was to win the day in his soul.

Narrator 4 Through the naked hallway into the kitchen. A group of his brothers and sisters was sitting round the table

Sister Tea's nearly over.

Narrator 4 Only the last of the second watered tea remained. Discarded crusts and lumps of sugared bread lay scattered. Little wells of tea here and there on the board, and a knife with a broken ivory handle was stuck through the pith of a ravaged turnover.

Stephen 4 Where are they?

Sister Goneboro toboro lookboro atboro aboro houseboro.

Stephen 4 Why are we on the move again if it's a fair question?

Brother Becauseboro theboro landboro lordboro willboro putboro usboro outboro.

Sister Singboro itboro againboro.

Brother (*sings Oft in the Stilly Night*)
Oft in the stilly night,
Ere Slumber's chain has bound me,
Fond Memory brings the light
Of other days around me;
The smiles, the tears,
Of boyhood's years,
The words of love then spoken;
The eyes that shone,
Now dimm'd and gone,
The cheerful hearts now broken!
Thus, in the stilly night,
Ere Slumber's chain hath bound me,
Sad Memory brings the light
Of other days around me.

The stage is bathed in bright light.

Narrator 4   All through your boyhood you had mused upon that which you had so often thought to be your destiny and when the moment had come for you to obey the call you had turned aside, obeying a wayward instinct. Now time lay between: the oils of ordination would never anoint your body. You had refused. Why?

Crossing the wooden bridge at Dollymount, you felt the planks shaking with the tramp of heavily shod feet. A squad of Christian brothers was on its way back from The Bull and had begun to pass, two by two, across the bridge. Soon the whole bridge was trembling and resounding. The uncouth faces passed, two by two. You drew forth a phrase from your treasure.

Stephen 4   A day of dappled seaborne clouds.

Bathers   Hello, Stephanos!

Here comes the Dedalus!

Ao! . . . Eh, give it over, Dwyer, I'm telling you, or I'll give you a stuff in the kisser for yourself . . . Ao!

Good man, Towser! Duck him!

Come along, Dedalus!

Duck him! Guzzle him now, Towser!

Help! Help! . . . Ao!

Narrator 4   The mere sight of that medley wet nakedness chilled you to the bone. A pain to see them, and a swordlike pain to see the signs of adolescence that made repellent their pitiable nakedness.

Bather   Stephanos Dedalos!

Narrator 4   Now, as never before, your strange name seemed a prophecy. Now, at the name of the fabulous artificer, you seem to hear the noise of dim waves and to see a winged form flying above the waves and slowly climbing the air.

Bather   One! Two! . . . Look out!

O, Cripes, I'm drownded!

One! Two! Three and away!

Narrator 4   Your throat was aching with a desire to cry aloud –

Stephen 4   To cry piercingly of my deliverance to the winds. –

Narrator 4   An instant of wild flight. Soul arisen from the grave of boyhood, spurning her grave-clothes. You were alone, unheeded, happy and near to the wild heart of life.

Stephen 4   Alone and young and wilful and wildhearted, alone amid a waste of wild air and brackish waters and the sea-harvest of shells and tangle and veiled grey sunlight and gayclad lightclad figures of children and girls and voices childish and girlish in the air.

He turns to see a girl, barefoot, ahead of him (played by the actress who played **Emma***).*

Narrator 4   The girl stood, alone and still, gazing out to sea, like one whom magic had changed into the likeness of a strange and beautiful seabird. Her long slender bare legs were delicate as a crane's, and pure save where an emerald trail of seaweed had fashioned itself as a sign upon the flesh.

Stephen 4   The white fringes of her drawers like feathering of soft white down.

Narrator 4   Her slate-blue skirts, kilted boldly about her waist and dovetailed behind her. Her bosom was as a bird's, soft and slight –

Stephen 4   – slight and soft as the breast of some dark-plumaged dove.

Narrator 4   But her long fair hair was girlish: and girlish, and touched with the wonder of mortal beauty –

Narrator 4/Stephen 4   – her face.

Narrator 4   She was alone and still –

Stephen 4   – gazing out to sea –

Narrator 4   – and when she felt your presence and the worship of your eyes her eyes turned to you in quiet sufferance of your gaze –

Stephen 4   – without shame or wantonness.

Narrator 4   Long, long she suffered your gaze and then quietly withdrew her eyes from yours and bent them towards the stream –

Stephen 4   – gently stirring the water with her foot hither and thither.

Narrator 4   The first faint noise of gently moving water broke the silence –

Stephen 4   – low and faint and whispering, faint as the bells of sleep –

Narrator 4   – hither and thither –

Stephen 4   – hither and thither –

Narrator 4   – and a faint flame trembled on her cheek.

Narrator 4/Stephen 4   Heavenly God!

Scene Threee

Stephen 4 *has disappeared.* **Emma/Bird-Girl** *is now* **Stephen 5**. *There is a new narrator,* **Narrator 5**. **Stephen**'s *mother brings on a wash-basin.* **Stephen** *leafs through a handful of papers.*

Narrator 5   One pair buskins.
One dress coat.
Three articles and white.
One man's pants.

Stephen 5   Pawn dockets?

May   Leave them.

She takes the dockets from him.

Stephen 5   How much is the clock fast now?

May   An hour and twenty-five minutes. The right time now
is twenty past ten. The dear knows you might try to be in
time for your lectures.

Katey, fill out the place for your brother to wash.

It's a poor case when a university student is so dirty that his
mother has to wash him.

Stephen 5   But it gives you pleasure.

May   I must try and get in to town tomorrow in time for
High Mass in Marlborough St. Tomorrow is a great feast day
in the Church.

Stephen 5   Why?

May   The Ascension of Our Lord.

Stephen 5   And why is that a great feast day?

May   On that day he showed Himself Divine: he ascended
into Heaven.

Stephen 5   Where did he go off?

May   From Mount Olivet.

Stephen 5   Head first?

May   Stephen! I'm afraid you have lost your faith.

Stephen 5   I'm afraid so too.

A shrill whistle from upstairs.

May   Dry yourself and hurry out for the love of goodness.

Another whistle. **Stephen**'s **Sister** *enters.*

Sister   Yes, Father?

Simon   Is your lazy bitch of a brother gone out yet?

Sister   Yes, Father.

Simon   Sure?

Sister   Yes, Father.

May   Ah, it's a scandalous shame for you, Stephen, and you'll live to rue the day you set your foot in that place. I know how it has changed you.

Stephen   Good morning everybody.

Scene Four

The Mad Nun Screams: 'Jesus, Jesus, Jesus!'

Narrator 5   A mad nun, screeching in the nuns' madhouse beyond the wall . . . His father's whistle, his mother's mutterings, the screech of an unseen maniac were so many voices offending and threatening to humble the pride of his youth. Then the rain-laden trees of the avenue evoked in him, as always –

Stephen 5   – memories of the girls and women in the plays of Gerhart Hauptmann.

Narrator 5   He foreknew that as he passed the sloblands of Fairview he would think of –

Stephen 5   – the cloistral silver-veined prose of Newman.

Narrator 5   Along the North Strand Road, glancing idly at the windows of the provision shops –

Stephen 5   – the dark humour of Guido Cavalcanti.

Narrator 5   Going by Baird's stonecutting works in Talbot Place the spirit of Ibsen would blow through him like a keen wind.

Stephen 5   Eleven! Late for that lecture too then.

Narrator 5   What day of the week was it? Thursday.

Stephen 5   Ten to eleven, English; eleven to twelve, French; twelve to one, physics.

Narrator 5   Passing a grimy marine dealer's shop beyond the Liffey –

Stephen 5   – the dainty songs of the Elizabethans!

Narrator 5   The grey block of Trinity on his left –

Stephen 5   – set heavily in the city's ignorance like a dull stone set in a cumbrous ring.

Narrator 5   The droll statue of Moore –

Stephen 5   – the 'national poet of Ireland'.

Narrator 5   It seemed humbly conscious of its indignity. He thought of his friend Davin, the peasant student.

Davin *joins* **Stephen.**

Davin   Peasant student? Go on, Stevie, call me what you will.

Narrator 5   Stevie. The homely version of his Christian name touched Stephen pleasantly.

Davin   A thing happened to myself, Stevie, last autumn, coming on winter, and I never told it to a living soul and you are the first person now I ever told it to. It was before I came up here. I was away all that day at a hurling match. My first cousin, Fonsy Davin, was stripped to his buff that day minding cúl for the Limericks but he was up with the forwards half the time and shouting like mad. One of the Crokes made a woeful wipe at him one time with his caman and I declare to God he was within an aim's ace of getting it at the side of his temple. Oh, honest to God, if the crook of it caught him that time he was done for.

Stephen 5   I am glad he escaped, but surely that's not the strange thing that happened to you?

Davin   I missed the train home so there was nothing for it only to stay the night or to foot it out. Well, I started to walk and it was coming on night. You wouldn't see the sign of a Christian house along the road or hear a sound. It was pitch dark almost. At last, after a bend of the road, I spied a little cottage with a light in the window. I went up and knocked at the door. A voice asked who was there and I answered and that I'd be thankful for a glass of water. After a while a young woman opened the door and brought me out a big mug of milk. She was half undressed as if she was going to bed and she had her hair hanging and I thought by her figure and by something in the look of her eyes that she must be carrying a child. She kept me in talk a long while at the door, and I thought it strange because her breast and her shoulders were bare. She asked me was I tired and would I like to stop the night there. She said she was all alone in the house and that her husband had gone that morning to Queenstown with his sister to see her off. And all the time she was talking, Stevie, she had her eyes fixed on my face and she stood so close to me I could hear her breathing. When I handed her back the mug at last she took my hand to draw me in over the threshold and said:

Davin/Emma   Come in and stay the night here. You've no call to be frightened. There's no one in it but ourselves.

Davin   I didn't go in, Stevie. I thanked her and went on my way again, all in a fever. At the first bend of the road I looked back and she was standing at the door.

Narrator 5   A type of her race –

Stephen 5   – and of my own –

Narrator 5   A bat-like soul waking to the consciousness of itself in darkness and secrecy and loneliness.

Stephen *continues his walk.*

Flower Girl   Ah, gentleman, your own girl, sir! The first handsel today, gentleman. Buy that lovely bunch. Will you, gentleman? Do, gentleman! Don't forget your own girl, sir!

Stephen 5   I have no money.

Flower Girl   Buy them lovely ones, will you, sir? Only a penny.

Stephen 5   Did you hear what I said? I told you I had no money. I tell you again now.

Flower Girl   Well, sure, you will some day, sir, please God.

Stephen 5   Possibly, but I don't think it likely.

Narrator 5   At the head of Grafton Street a slab was set to the memory of Wolfe Tone and he remembered having been present with his father at its laying. Entering the sombre college, too late to go upstairs to the French class. The corridor dark and silent. The Ireland of Tone and of Parnell seemed to have receded in space.

Scene Five

Stephen *approaches the* **Dean of Studies***, who is working on a fire.*

Stephen 5   Good morning, sir! Can I help you?

Narrator 5   He opened the door of the lecture theatre. The Dean of Studies was crouching before the large grate.

Dean   One moment now, Mr Dedalus, and you will see. There is an art in lighting a fire. We have the liberal arts and we have the useful arts. This is one of the useful arts.

Stephen 5   I will try to learn it.

Dean   Not too much coal, that is one of the secrets.

Stephen 5   I am sure I could not light a fire.

Dean You are an artist, are you not, Mr Dedalus? The object of the artist is the creation of the beautiful. What the beautiful is, is another question. Can you solve that question now?

Stephen 5 *Aquinas says pulcra sunt quae visa placent.*

Dean 'That is beautiful which gives pleasure to the eye.' This fire before us will be pleasing to the eye. Will it therefore be beautiful?

Stephen 5 In so far as it is apprehended by the sight, which I suppose means here aesthetic intellection, it will be beautiful. But Aquinas also says *bonum est in quod tendit appetitus.*

Dean 'The good is in that toward which the appetite tends.'

Stephen 5 In so far as it satisfies the animal craving for warmth fire is a good. In hell, however, it is an evil.

Dean Quite so, you have certainly hit the nail on the head.

Narrator 5 The Dean rose nimbly, went to the door and set it ajar.

Dean A draught is said to be a help in these matters. When may we expect to have something from you on the aesthetic question?

Stephen 5 From me! I stumble on an idea once a fortnight if I am lucky.

Dean These questions are very profound, Mr Dedalus. It is like looking down from the cliffs of Moher into the depths. Many go down into the depths and never come up.

Stephen 5 For my purpose I can work on at present by the light of one or two ideas of Aristotle and Aquinas.

Dean I see. I quite see your point.

Stephen 5 I need them only for my own use and guidance until I have done something for myself by their light. If the lamp doesn't give light enough I shall sell it and buy another.

Dean   The feeding of the lamp is also a nice problem. You must choose the pure oil and you must be careful when you pour it in not to overflow it, not to pour in more than the funnel can hold.

Stephen 5   What funnel?

Dean   The funnel through which you pour the oil into your lamp.

Stephen 5   That? Is that called a funnel? Is it not a tundish?

Dean   What is a tundish?

Stephen 5   That. The . . . funnel.

Dean   Is that called a tundish in Ireland? I never heard the word in my life.

Together, **Narrator 5** *and* **Stephen 5** *laugh mockingly.*

Stephen 5   It is called a tundish in Lower Drumcondra, where they speak the best English.

Dean   A tundish. That is a most interesting word. I must look that word up. Upon my word I must. Tundish! Well now, that is interesting!

Stephen 5   The question you asked me a moment ago seems to me more interesting. What is that beauty which the artist struggles to express from lumps of earth?

Dean   And to distinguish between the beautiful and the sublime, to distinguish between moral beauty and material beauty.

Narrator 5   The language in which we are speaking is his before it is mine.

Dean   And to inquire what kind of beauty is proper to each of the various arts. In pursuing these speculations, there is, however, the danger of perishing of inanition.

Narrator 5   How different are the words home, Christ, ale, master, on his lips and on mine!

Dean   First you must take your degree.

Narrator 5   His language, so familiar and so foreign, will always be for me an acquired speech.

Dean   Set that before you as your first aim. Then, little by little, you will see your way. I mean in every sense, your way in life and in thinking.

Narrator 5   I have not made or accepted its words. My voice holds them at bay. My soul frets in the shadow of his language.

Dean   It may be uphill pedalling at first. Take Simon Moonan. He was a long time before he got to the top. But he got there.

Stephen 5   I may not have his talent.

Dean   You never know. We never can say what is in us.

He exits.

Scene Six

McCann *has entered and set up a little table, on which is a petition.* **Students** *enter and sign.*

McCann   Sign the petition! Universal peace! Universal suffrage! Secure as cheaply as possible the greatest possible happiness of the greatest possible number.

Temple   Three cheers for universal brotherhood! MacCann is in tiptop form. Ready to shed the last drop. Brand new world. No stimulants and votes for the bitches.

Stephen 5 (*to* **Cranly**, *of the student*)   Perhaps you can tell me why he pours his soul so freely into my ear. Can you?

Cranly   A sugar. A flaming bloody sugar, that's what he is!

Narrator 5   Cranly's epitaph for all dead friendships. Would it ever be spoken in the same tone over Stephen's memory?

Stephen 5   Have you signed?

Cranly   *Ego habeo . . .*

Stephen 5   Pfft!

Cranly   Are you annoyed?

Stephen 5   No.

Cranly   Are you in bad humour?

Stephen 5   No.

McCann   You'll sign the testimonial?

Stephen 5   Will you pay me anything if I sign?

McCann   Minor poets, I suppose, are above such trivial questions as universal peace.

Stephen 5   My signature is of no account. You are right to go your way. Leave me to go mine.

Temple   By hell, that's a good one! I like that expression immensely.

Cranly   Temple, I declare to the living God if you say another word to anybody on any subject, I'll kill you super spottum.

Temple   I don't care a damn about you, Cranly. (*Of* **Stephen**.) *He's* the only man I see in this institution that has an individual mind.

Cranly   Institution! Individual! Go home, blast you, for you're a hopeless bloody man.

Temple *goes off as* **Lynch** *and* **Davin** *enter.*

Cranly   A flaming, flaring, bloody idiot. Did you ever see such a go-by-the-wall?

Lynch *laughs.*

Cranly   Lynch is awake.

Stephen 5   Lynch puts out his chest, as a criticism of life.

Lynch   Who has anything to say about my girth?

Cranly *and* **Lynch** *run off, in a mock tussle.*

Stephen 5 *(to Davin)*   Did you sign McCann's petition?

Davin *nods.*

Davin   And you, Stevie?

Stephen *shakes his head.*

Davin   You're a terrible man, Stevie, always alone.

Stephen 5   Now that you have signed the petition for universal peace, I suppose you'll burn that little copybook I saw in your room.

Davin   Eh?

Stephen 5   Long pace, fianna! Right incline, fianna! Fianna, by numbers, salute, one, two!

Davin   You're a born sneerer, Stevie.

Stephen 5   When you make the next rebellion with hurleysticks, and want the indispensable informer, tell me. I can find you a few in this college.

Davin   I can't understand you. One time I hear you talk against English literature. Now you talk against the Irish informers. What with your name and your ideas – are you Irish at all? Why don't you learn Irish? Why did you drop out of the league class after the first lesson?

Stephen 5   You know one reason why.

Davin   Is it on account of that certain young lady and Father Moran? That's all in your own mind, Stevie. He and Emma were only talking and laughing.

Narrator 5   All in your own mind. That last meeting at the Christmas party. The dance brought her close.

Emma *dances across to* **Stephen.** *They dance together.*

Emma   You are a great stranger now.

Stephen 5   Yes, I was born to be a monk.

Emma   I am afraid you are a heretic.

Stephen 5   Are you much afraid?

Emma   I want to hear you sing again.

Stephen 5   O, thanks . . . Some time, perhaps . . .

Emma   Have you ever heard Father Moran sing?

Stephen 5   No. Has he a good voice?

Emma   O, very nice.

Stephen 5   Do you go to confession to him?

Emma   Now, don't be bold, Stephen.

Stephen 5   I wish you would go to confession to me, Emma.

Emma   That's a dreadful thing to say . . . Why would you like that?

Stephen 5   To hear your sins.

Emma   Stephen!

Stephen 5   To hear you murmur them into my ear and say you were sorry and would never commit them again and ask me to forgive you. And I would forgive you and make you promise to commit them every time you liked and say 'God bless you, my dear child.'

Emma   O, for shame, Stephen! You'd get tired of that too.

Narrator 5/Stephen 5   Do you think so?

She goes; **Stephen** *watches her a moment, then turns to* **Davin**.

Stephen 5   Davin, do you remember when we knew each other first? The first morning we met you asked me to show you the way to the *ma*-triculation class, you remember? I ask myself: is he as innocent as his speech?

Davin   I'm a simple person. You know that. When you told me that night in Harcourt Street those things about your private life, honest to God, Stevie, I wasn't able to eat my dinner.

Stephen 5   Thanks. You mean I am a monster.

Davin   No. But I wish you hadn't told me.

Stephen 5   This race and this country and this life produced me. I shall express myself as I am.

Davin   Try to be one of us. In heart you are an Irish man but your pride is too powerful.

Stephen 5   My ancestors threw off their language and took another. They allowed a handful of foreigners to subject them. Do you fancy I am going to pay in my own life and person debts they made? What for?

Davin   For our freedom.

Stephen 5   No honourable and sincere man has given up to you his life and his youth and his affections from the days of Tone to those of Parnell, but you sold him to the enemy or failed him in need or reviled him and left him for another. And you invite me to be one of you. I'd see you damned first.

Davin   They died for their ideals, Stevie. Our day will come yet, believe me.

Stephen 5   The soul has a slow and dark birth, more mysterious than the birth of the body. When the soul of a man is born in this country there are nets flung at it to hold it back from flight. You talk to me of nationality, language, religion. I shall try to fly by those nets.

Davin   You mean, fly, using those nets?

Stephen 5   I meant fly past them, but . . .

He shrugs, a concession that either meaning might work.

Davin   Too deep for me, Stevie. But a man's country comes first. Ireland first, Stevie. You can be a poet or a mystic after.

Stephen 5   Do you know what Ireland is? Ireland is the old sow that eats her farrow.

Cranly *and* **Lynch** *return,* **Cranly** *bouncing a handball.*

Cranly   Here Davin, give us a game.

Davin *shakes his head at* **Stephen.** *Goes off with* **Cranly.**
Stephen *hands* **Lynch** *a cigarette*

Scene Seven

Stephen 5   I know you are poor.

Lynch   Damn your yellow insolence.

Stephen 5   It was a great day for European culture when you made up your mind to swear in yellow.

They both light up.

I have defined the aesthetic emotion as static.

Lynch   Stop! I won't listen! I am sick. I was out last night on a yellow drunk with Horan and Goggins.

Stephen 5   The aesthetic emotion is static. The feelings excited by improper art are kinetic: desire or loathing.

Lynch   So art must not excite desire? I told you that one day I wrote my name in pencil on the backside of the Venus of Praxiteles in the Museum. Was that not desire?

Stephen 5   I speak of normal natures. You also told me that when you were a boy you ate pieces of dried cowdung.

Lynch   O, I did! I did! Remember, though, that I admire only beauty. Let me hear what you call beauty.

Stephen *awkwardly puts his hand on* **Lynch**'s *shoulder.*

Stephen 5   We are right, and the others are wrong. To speak of these things and to try to understand their nature.

Lynch   Out with another definition.

Stephen 5   Aquinas says that is beautiful the apprehension of which pleases.

Lynch   It amuses me vastly to hear you quoting Aquinas time after time like a jolly round friar. Are you laughing in your sleeve?

Narrator 5   A fine rain fell from the high-veiled sky.

Emma *and some others gather to shelter from the rain.* **Cranly** *is there too.*

Lynch   Your beloved is here.

Stephen 5 (*ignoring this*)   I have a book at home in which I have written down questions more amusing than yours. In finding the answers to them I found the theory of aesthetic which I am trying to explain. Is a chair finely made tragic or comic? Is the portrait of the Mona Lisa good if I desire to see it? If not, why not?

Lynch   Why not, indeed?

Stephen 5   If a man hacking in fury at a block of wood, make there an image of a cow, is that image a work of art? If not, why not?

Lynch   That's a lovely one. That has the true scholastic stink.

Narrator 5   She has no priest to flirt with.

Stephen 5   The personality of the artist refines itself out of existence, impersonalises itself, so to speak. The artist, like the God of creation, remains within or behind or beyond or above his handiwork, invisible, refined out of existence, indifferent, paring his fingernails.

Lynch   Trying to refine them also out of existence.

Two **Students** *pass.*

Student 1   An Irish country practice is best. Hynes was two years in Liverpool and says the same. A frightful hole he said it was. Nothing but midwifery cases.

Student 2   Hynes has no brains. He got through by stewing, pure stewing. Don't mind him. There's plenty of money to be made in big commercial city.

Student 1   Depends on the practice.

Lynch   What do you mean by prating about beauty and the imagination in this miserable godforsaken island? No wonder the artist retired within or behind his handiwork after having perpetrated this country.

He goes.

Stephen 5   She was preparing to go away. The quick light shower had drawn off, tarrying in clusters of diamonds among the shrubs where an exhalation was breathed forth by the blackened earth.

Cranly, **Emma** *and her friend go. A look between* **Emma** *and* **Cranly**. *She looks at* **Stephen**, *who very deliberately looks away.* **Emma** *and friend exit.*

Narrator 5   Was there a slight flush on Cranly's cheek? Did that explain his listless silence, his harsh comments?

Cranly   Why was it that when he thought of Cranly he could never raise before his mind the entire image of his body but only the image of the head and face?

Stephen 5   Well, let her go, and be damned to her!

Narrator 5   And if he had judged her harshly? If her life were a simple rosary of hours, her life simple and strange as a bird's life, gay in the morning, restless all day, tired at sundown? Her heart simple and wilful as a bird's heart?

Scene Eight

Emma   Towards dawn he awoke. O what sweet music! His soul all dewy wet. Over his limbs in sleep pale cool waves of light had passed. He lay still, as if his soul lay amid cool waters, conscious of faint sweet music. His mind was waking slowly to a tremulous morning knowledge, a morning inspiration. A spirit filled him, pure as the purest water, sweet as dew, moving as music. The night had been enchanted. In a dream or vision he had known the ecstasy of seraphic life. An instant of enchantment only or long hours and years and ages?

Stephen *begins to write.* **Stephen 1** *appears and goes and sits on one of the benches.*

Stephen 1
> Are you not weary of ardent ways,
> Lure of the fallen seraphim?
> Tell no more of enchanted days.

Narrator 5   He wrote verses for her again after ten years. The verses passed from his mind to his lips, and he felt the rhythmic movement of a villanelle pass through them.

Stephen 2 *appears.*

Stephen 2
> A rose and ardent glow,

Narrator 5
> Which sent forth rays of rhyme;

Stephen 5   Ways, days, blaze, praise, raise . . .

Narrator 5   Its rays burned up the world, consumed the hearts of men and angels.

Stephen 5
> Your eyes have set man's heart ablaze
> And you have had your will of him.

Stephen 1   Are you not weary of ardent ways?

Narrator 5   Then, smoke, incense ascending from the altar of the world.

Stephen 3 *enters, kneels by the desks.*

Stephen 3
Above the flame the smoke of praise
Goes up from ocean rim to rim.

Stephen 2   Tell no more of enchanted days.

Narrator 5   The earth like a swinging swaying censer, a
ball of incense. He pictured Father Moran . . .

Father Moran   'The ladies are coming round to us. I can
see it every day.'

Stephen 5   A priested peasant.

Father Moran   'The ladies are with us. The best helpers
the language has.'

Narrator 5   But then . . . then the radiant image of the
eucharist united in an instant all his bitter thoughts, their cries
arising in a hymn of thanksgiving.

Now the five **Stephens** *and* **Narrator** *follow each other around
the stage, in an elaborate, dance-like movement.*

Stephen 3
Our broken cries and mournful lays
Rise in one eucharistic hymn . . .

Stephen 1 *and* **2**   Are you not weary of ardent ways?

Stephen 5
Are you not weary of ardent ways,
Lure of the fallen seraphim?

Stephen 2   Tell no more of enchanted days.

Stephen 3
Your eyes have set man's heart ablaze
And you have had your will of him.
Stephen 1   Are you not weary of ardent ways?

Stephen 3
Above the flame the smoke of praise
Goes up from ocean rim to rim.

Stephen 2
Tell no more of enchanted days.

Stephen 5
Our broken cries and mournful lays
Rise in one eucharistic hymn.

Stephen 1, 2 *and* **3**
Are you not weary of ardent ways?

Stephen 4
While sacrificing hands upraise
The chalice flowing to the brim.

Stephen 1, 2 *and* **3**
Tell no more of enchanted days.

Stephen 3
And still you hold our longing gaze

Stephen 5
With languorous look and lavish limb!

All   Are you not weary of ardent ways?
Tell no more of enchanted days.

Narrator 5   If he sent her the verses? They would be read out at breakfast amid the tapping of egg shells. Her brothers would laugh and try to wrest the page from each other with their strong hard fingers. The suave priest, her uncle, seated in his armchair, would hold the page at arm's length, read it smiling and approve of the literary form.

Stephens 1, 2 *and* **3** *leave.* **Stephen 5** *makes a dismissive snort. Looks up.*

Scene Nine

Cranly *appears.* **Stephen** *rises to join him.*

Stephen 5   Cranly, come away.

Cranly   Now?

Stephen 5   I wanted to speak to you. I had an unpleasant quarrel this evening.

Cranly   With your people?

Stephen 5   With my mother.

Cranly   About religion?

Stephen 5   Yes.

Cranly   What age is your mother?

Stephen 5   Not old. She wishes me to make my Easter duty.

Cranly   And will you?

Stephen 5   I will not.

Cranly   Why not?

Stephen 5   I will not serve.

Cranly   That remark was made before.

Stephen 5   It is made behind now.

Cranly   Do you believe in the eucharist?

Stephen 5   I do not.

Cranly   Do you disbelieve then?

Stephen 5   I neither believe in it nor disbelieve in it.

Cranly   Many persons have doubts, even religious persons, yet they overcome them or put them aside. Are your doubts too strong?

Stephen 5   I do not wish to overcome them. Don't, please. You cannot discuss this question with your mouth full of chewed fig.

Cranly (*spits out fig*)   Depart from me, ye cursed, into everlasting fire! Do you not fear that those words may be spoken to you on the Day of Judgement?

Stephen 5   What is offered me on the other hand? An eternity of bliss in the company of the Dean of Studies?

Cranly   It is a curious thing, do you know, how your mind is supersaturated with the religion in which you say you disbelieve. Did you believe in it when you were at school? I bet you did.

Stephen 5   I did.

Cranly   And were you happier then? Happier than you are now, for instance?

Stephen 5   Often happy, and often unhappy. I was someone else then.

Cranly   How someone else? What do you mean by that statement?

Stephen 5   I mean that I was not myself as I am now, as I had to become.

Cranly   'Not as you are now, not as you had to become.' Let me ask you a question. Do you love your mother?

Stephen 5   I don't know what your words mean.

Cranly   Have you never loved anyone?

Stephen 5   Do you mean women?

Cranly   I am not speaking of that. I ask you if you ever felt love towards anyone or anything?

Stephen 5   I tried to love God. It seems now I failed.

Cranly   Has your mother had a happy life?

Stephen 5   How do I know?

Cranly   How many children had she?

Stephen 5   Nine or ten. Some died.

Cranly   Was your father . . . I don't want to pry into your family affairs. But was your father what is called well-to-do? I mean, when you were growing up?

Stephen 5   Yes.

Cranly   What was he?

Stephen 5   A medical student, an oarsman, a tenor, an amateur actor, a shouting politician, a small landlord, a small investor, a drinker, a good fellow, a storyteller, somebody's secretary, something in a distillery, a tax-gatherer, a bankrupt and at present a praiser of his own past.

Cranly   The distillery is damn good.

Stephen 5   Is there anything else you want to know?

Cranly   Are you in good circumstances at present?

Stephen 5   Do I look it?

Cranly   So then, you were born 'in the lap of luxury'. Your mother must have gone through a good deal of suffering. Would you not try to save her from suffering more even if . . . or would you?

Stephen 5   If I could, that would cost me very little.

Cranly   Then do so. Do as she wishes you to do. What is it for you? You disbelieve in it. It is a form: nothing else. And you will set her mind at rest. Whatever else is unsure in this stinking dunghill of a world a mother's love is not. Your mother brings you into the world, carries you first in her body. What do we know about what she feels? But whatever she feels, it, at least, must be real. It must be. What are our ideas or ambitions? Play. Ideas! Every jackass going the roads thinks he has ideas.

Stephen 5   Pascal, if I remember rightly, would not suffer his mother to kiss him as he feared the contact of her sex.

Cranly   Pascal was a pig.

Stephen 5   Aloysius Gonzaga, I think, was of the same mind.

Cranly   And he was another pig then.

Stephen 5   The Church calls him a saint.

Cranly   I don't care a flaming damn what anyone calls him. I call him a pig.

Stephen 5   Jesus, too, seems to have treated his mother with scant courtesy in public.

Cranly   Did the idea ever occur to you that Jesus was not what he pretended to be?

Stephen 5   The first person to whom that idea occurred was Jesus himself.

Cranly   I mean, did the idea ever occur to you that he was himself a conscious hypocrite, what he called the Jews of his time, a whited sepulchre? Or, to put it more plainly, that he was a blackguard?

Stephen 5   That idea never occurred to me.

Cranly   Tell me the truth. Were you at all shocked by what I said?

Stephen 5   Somewhat.

Cranly   And why were you shocked, if you feel sure that our religion is false and that Jesus was not the son of God?

Stephen 5   I am not at all sure of it. He is more like a son of God than a son of Mary.

Cranly   And is that why you will not take communion, because you feel that the host, too, may be the body and blood of the son of God and not a wafer of bread? And because you fear that it may be?

Stephen 5   Yes, I feel that and I also fear it.

Cranly   I see.

Stephen 5   I fear many things: dogs, horses, firearms, the sea, thunderstorms, machinery, the country roads at night.

Cranly   But why do you fear a bit of bread?

Stephen 5   I imagine that there is a malevolent reality behind those things I say I fear.

Cranly   Do you fear then that the God of the Roman Catholics would strike you dead and damn you if you made a sacrilegious communion?

Stephen 5   The God of the Roman Catholics could do that now. I fear more than that the chemical action which would be set up in my soul by a false homage to a symbol behind which are massed twenty centuries of authority and veneration.

Cranly   Would you, asked, in extreme danger, commit that particular sacrilege? For instance, if you lived in the penal days?

Stephen 5   I cannot answer for the past. Possibly not.

Cranly   Then you do not intend to become a Protestant?

Stephen 5   I said that I had lost the faith, but not that I had lost self-respect. What kind of liberation would that be to forsake an absurdity which is logical and coherent and to embrace one which is illogical and incoherent?

Narrator 5 *moves towards* **Stephen**. *Puts his hand on his shoulder.* **Stephen 5** *looks at him, nods.*

Stephen 5   Probably I shall go away.

Cranly   Where?

Stephen 5   Where I can.

Cranly   Yes. It might be difficult for you to live here now. But is it that makes you go?

Stephen 5   I have to go.

Cranly   There are many good believers who think as you do. Would that surprise you? The Church is not the stone building nor even the clergy and their dogmas. It is the whole mass of those born into it.

Stephen 5   I will not serve that in which I no longer believe, whether it call itself my home, my fatherland, or my church: and I will try to express myself in some mode of life or art as freely as I can and as wholly as I can, using for my defence the only arms I allow myself to use – silence, exile, and cunning.

Cranly   Cunning indeed! Is it you? You poor poet, you!

Stephen 5   And you made me confess to you, as I have confessed to you so many other things, have I not?

Cranly   Yes, my child.

Stephen 5   You made me confess the fears that I have. But I will tell you also what I do not fear. I do not fear to be alone or to be spurned for another or to leave whatever I have to leave. And I am not afraid to make a mistake, even a great mistake, a lifelong mistake, and perhaps as long as eternity too.

Cranly   Alone, quite alone. You have no fear of that. And you know what that word means? Not only to be separate from all others but to have not even one friend.

Stephen 5   I will take the risk.

Cranly   And not to have any one person, who would be more than a friend, more even than the noblest and truest friend a man ever had.

Stephen 5   Of whom are you speaking?

Blackout.

Scene Ten

Stephen 5 *is packing books into his suitcase. The dates are announced by other cast members.*

Cranly   March 20th.

Stephen 5   Long talk with Cranly on the subject of my revolt. He had his grand manner on. I supple and suave. Attacked me on the score of love for one's mother. Tried to imagine his mother: cannot.

Dante   March 21st.

Stephen 5   Free. Soulfree and fancyfree. Let the dead bury the dead. Aye, and let the dead marry the dead.

May   March 24th.

Stephen 5   Began with a discussion with my mother. Subject: Blessed Virgin Mary. Handicapped by my sex and youth. Mother indulgent. Said I have a queer mind and have read too much. Not true. Have read little and understood less. Then she said I would come back to faith because I had a restless mind. This means to leave church by back door of sin and re-enter through the skylight of repentance. Cannot repent. Told her so and asked for sixpence. Got threepence.

Then went to college. Crossing Stephen's, that is, my green, went to library. Tried to read three reviews. Useless. She is not out yet. Am I alarmed? About what? That she will never be out again.

Emma   April 2nd.

Stephen 5   Saw her drinking tea and eating cakes in Johnston's, Mooney and O'Brien's. Rather, lynx-eyed Lynch saw her as we passed. He tells me Cranly was invited there by brother. Is he the shining light now?

Davin   April 3rd.

Stephen 5   Davin asked me was it true I was going away and why. Told him the shortest way to Tara was via Holyhead. Just then my father came up. Introduction. Father polite and observant. Asked Davin if he might offer him some refreshment. Davin could not, was going to a meeting. When we came away Father told me he had a good honest eye. Asked me why I did not join a rowing club. I pretended to think it over.

Stephen 4   April 5th.

Stephen 5   Wild spring. Scudding clouds. O life! Dark stream of swirling bogwater on which apple trees have cast down their delicate flowers. Eyes of girls among the leaves. Girls demure and romping. All fair or auburn: no dark ones. They blush better. Houpla!

Lynch   April 6th.

Stephen 5   Certainly she remembers the past. Lynch says all women do. Then she remembers the time of her childhood – and mine, if I was ever a child. The past is consumed in the present and the present is living only because it brings forth the future.

He finds a book and reads.

'When my arms wrap around you I press
My heart upon the loveliness
That has long faded from the world . . .'

Phh! Not this, Mr Yeats. Not at all. I desire to press in my arms the loveliness which has not yet come into the world.

Dean   April 13th.

Stephen 5   That tundish has been on my mind for a long time . . . Tundish! English and good old blunt English too. Damn the Dean of Studies and his funnel! What did he come here for to teach us his own language or to learn it from us. Damn him one way or the other!.

Emma   April 15th.

Stephen 5   Met her today point blank in Grafton Street. The crowd brought us together. We both stopped. She asked me why I never came, said she had heard all sorts of stories about me. This was only to gain time. Asked me was I writing poems? About whom? I asked her. This confused her more and I felt sorry and mean. Talked rapidly of myself and my plans. In the midst of it unluckily I made a sudden gesture of a revolutionary nature. I must have looked like a fellow throwing a handful of peas into the air. People began to look at us. She shook hands a moment after and, in going away, said she hoped I would do what I said.

Now I call that friendly, don't you?

Yes, I liked her today. A little or much? Don't know. I liked her and it seems a new feeling to me. Then all the rest, all that I thought I thought, and all that I felt I felt, all the rest before now, in fact . . . O, give it up, old chap! Sleep it off!

Stephen 1   April 16th.

Stephen 5   Away! Away! The spell of arms and voices: the white arms of roads, and the black arms of tall ships that stand against the moon, their tale of distant nations. They are held out to say: We are alone – come. We are your kinsmen. And the air is thick with their company as they call to me, their kinsman, making ready to go, shaking the wings of their exultant and terrible youth.

Stephen 4   April 26th.

Stephen 5   Mother is putting my new secondhand clothes in order. She prays now, she says, that I may learn in my own life and away from home and friends what the heart is and what it feels. Amen.

So be it. Welcome, O life, I go to encounter for the millionth time the reality of experience and to forge in the smithy of my soul the uncreated conscience of my race.

All   April 27th.

Old Father, old artificer, stand me now and ever in good stead.

End.

For a complete listing of
Methuen Drama titles, visit:

www.bloomsbury.com/drama

Follow us on Twitter and keep up to date
with our news and publications

@MethuenDrama